Intervention-based Research in Operations Management

Other titles in Foundations and Trends® in Technology, Information and Operations Management

Sequential Decision Analytics and Modeling: Modeling with Python
Warren B. Powell
ISBN: 978-1-63828-082-8

The Interface of Finance, Operations, and Risk Management
Volodymyr Babich and John R. Birge
ISBN: 978-1-68083-796-4

AI and Business Models: The Good, The Bad and The Ugly
Vania Sena and Manuela Nocker
ISBN: 978-1-68083-794-0

The Business of Electric Vehicles: A Platform Perspective
Jonas Boehm, Hemant K. Bhargava and Geoffrey G. Parker
ISBN: 978-1-68083-762-9

Advances in Supply Chain Finance and FinTech Innovations Overview
Panos Kouvelis, Ling Dong and Danko Turcic
ISBN: 978-1-68083-722-3

Intervention-based Research in Operations Management

Aravind Chandrasekaran
The Ohio State University
chandrasekaran.24@osu.edu

Rogelio Oliva
Texas A&M University
roliva@tamu.edu

Fabrizio Salvador
IE University
fabrizio.salvador@ie.edu

now
the essence of knowledge
Boston — Delft

Foundations and Trends® in Technology, Information and Operations Management

Published, sold and distributed by:
now Publishers Inc.
PO Box 1024
Hanover, MA 02339
United States
Tel. +1-781-985-4510
www.nowpublishers.com
sales@nowpublishers.com

Outside North America:
now Publishers Inc.
PO Box 179
2600 AD Delft
The Netherlands
Tel. +31-6-51115274

The preferred citation for this publication is

A. Chandrasekaran *et al.*. *Intervention-based Research in Operations Management*. Foundations and Trends® in Technology, Information and Operations Management, vol. 17, no. 1, pp. 1–81, 2023.

ISBN: 978-1-63828-224-2

Foundations and Trends® in Technology, Information and Operations Management

Volume 17, Issue 1, 2023

Editorial Board

Zuo-Jun Max Shen
University of California, Berkeley, USA

George Tagaras
Aristotle University of Thessaloniki, Greece

Sherri Xiaole Wu
Fudan University, China

Y. Karen Zheng
MIT, USA

Editorial Scope

Topics

Foundations and Trends® in Technology, Information and Operations Management publishes survey and tutorial articles in the following topics:

- B2B Commerce
- Business Process Engineering and Design
- Business Process Outsourcing
- Capacity Planning
- Competitive Operations
- Contracting in Supply Chains
- E-Commerce and E-Business Models
- Electronic markets, auctions and exchanges
- Enterprise Management Systems
- Facility Location
- Information Chain Structure and Competition
- International Operations
- Marketing/Manufacturing Interfaces
- Multi-location inventory theory
- New Product & Service Design
- Queuing Networks
- Reverse Logistics
- Service Logistics and Product Support
- Supply Chain Management
- Technology Management and Strategy
- Technology, Information and Operations in:
  - Automotive Industries
  - Electronics manufacturing
  - Financial Services
  - Health Care
  - Media and Entertainment
  - Process Industries
  - Retailing
  - Telecommunications

Information for Librarians

Foundations and Trends® in Technology, Information and Operations Management, 2023, Volume 17, 4 issues. ISSN paper version 1571-9545. ISSN online version 1571-9553. Also available as a combined paper and online subscription.

Contents

Intervention-based Research in Operations Management

Aravind Chandrasekaran[1], Rogelio Oliva[2] and Fabrizio Salvador[3]

[1]*Fisher College of Business, The Ohio State University, USA; chandrasekaran.24@osu.edu*
[2]*Mays Business School, Texas A&M University, USA; roliva@tamu.edu*
[3]*IE Business School, IE University, Madrid, Spain; fabrizio.salvador@ie.edu*

ABSTRACT

Intervention-Based Research (IBR) is a research method where scholars closely interact with practicing managers in understanding and solving complex problems, with the ultimate goal of generating novel theoretical insights. IBR calls for researchers to be actively involved in the problem-solving process, rather than observing it unobtrusively—as required by alternative approaches. IBR is particularly relevant and promising for Operations Management (OM) scholars, whose mission is to engage with practice to provide working solutions to operational problems. This fact is echoed in the rising interest among OM scholars for the application of IBR, the creation of IBR departments at the leading journals, as well as the publication of several articles using this novel research method. Yet researchers may struggle to find complete guidelines for designing and executing IBR projects. This monograph is meant to provide doctoral students and OM scholars with an overview of this

---

Aravind Chandrasekaran, Rogelio Oliva and Fabrizio Salvador (2023), "Intervention-based Research in Operations Management", Foundations and Trends® in Technology, Information and Operations Management: Vol. 17, No. 1, pp 1–81. DOI: 10.1561/0200000104.

research method. In Section 1, we make the case for the need for IBR, discuss its relation with engaged scholarship, and compare it with other commonly used research methods. In Section 2, we clarify the epistemological underpinnings of IBR by discussing how it supports abductive reasoning in theory building, and by exploring what is needed, from the researcher and the context situation, for IBR to yield theoretical insights. Section 3 outlines a typical process that researchers can follow when conducting IBR, presents strategies that researchers can take to reduce uncertainty and risks during their engagement, and illustrates some of the best practices that can lead to stronger engagement with the problem. Section 4 showcases recently published IBR papers in OM and uses these papers to help the reader grasp concrete examples of the fundamental methodological tenets of IBR. We conclude by synthesizing the threefold benefits of IBR of solving a problem from the field, generating theoretical insights, and educating aspiring managers on the problem and its solution.

Keywords: engaged scholarship; action research; problem-driven research; research methods.

1

Introduction to IBR[1]

Operations Management (OM) and management research in general have an old and thorny problem in that a preponderance of research articles emphasize theory development over providing advice to practitioners (Tranfield and Starkey, 1998; van de Ven and Johnson, 2006). Implications for practice are normally relegated to a shallow discussion, in the final section of a paper, of bold ideas about how organizations, individuals, or teams can benefit from the research. Such efforts to expound the practical implications of academic research are laudable but let us not fool ourselves; managers seldom read academic research articles, and when they do are unlikely to immediately implement any "practical" recommendations proffered therein. This is hardly surprising as a vast majority of recommendations are often speculative and devoid of pragmatic utility.

This problem is not new. Although researchers and practitioners in OM and other management disciplines have reiterated the need for academics to step out of their "ivory towers" and engage in problem-driven research (Eckhardt and Wetherbe, 2014; Tang, 2017; van Mieghem,

[1]The authors like to thank Professors Joan van Aken, Bradley Staats and Andrew van de Ven for their comments and thoughts in an earlier version of this section.

2013), few of us have done so. This disconnect between theory and practice poses a serious threat to effective teaching of OM to aspiring professionals. It constitutes a deplorable lost opportunity to support and improve the practice of OM and a hindrance to the creation of insightful research. The in-depth knowledge of recent and effective designs of OM processes and systems needed for effective teaching in OM needs to be provided by research. The intersection of research and practice, moreover, is the locus of opportunities to improve both theory and practice.

1.1 Purpose of Business School Research

The purpose of business school research must be understood in the broader context of academic research and its mission within university institutions. Until the XVI century, university teaching was heavily anchored to religious dogma and tradition set by earlier respected thinkers, as reflected in the so-called "ipse dixit" ("he himself, said it") principle. Starting from the XVII century enlightenment scholars rejected this traditional approach, and emphasized instead rationalism and empiricism (Descartes, 1998), according to which knowledge must be produced through observation and reflection (Locke, 1996). These ideas gained further traction in the XIX century, first in Germany and then in US universities, leading to the prescription of "unity of research and teaching" (Ashby, 1967): effective teaching had to be driven by rigorous academic research. This prescription gradually made its way into business schools, which had earlier deemphasized research in favor of a strong vocational focus. With the publication of the Ford and Carnegie Foundation reports (Gordon and Howell, 1959), business schools began a transformation from trade schools to research-based academic professional schools motivated by the primary objective of improving teaching quality. This improvement in teaching was to be based on research.

At this vital stage of business school development, Nobel laureate Herbert Simon proposed that the research agenda of business schools should strike a balance between rigor and pragmatism. He suggested that "the tasks of a business school are to train men (and women) for the practice of management (or some special branch of management) as a profession, and to develop new knowledge that may be relevant to improving the operation of business" (Simon, 1967, p. 1). Although this view reflected the abovementioned principle of "unity of research and teaching," Simon clarified that knowledge developed by business schools could include both general studies aimed at advancing fundamental knowledge and studies aimed at directly improving business practice (Simon, 1967, p. 1). These recommendations suggested that ideal research projects in business schools should combine a quest for fundamental understanding with considerations of use.

Unfortunately, business school research has seldom achieved this goal. Instead, much of the knowledge produced in business schools after the end of the Second World War has been developed without strong links to managerial practice, resulting in an inward focus on theory at the expense of practical relevance (van de Ven and Johnson, 2006). This gap between research and practice can undermine one of the key purposes of business school research, which is to support effective teaching and improve business practice. In other words, good theory should keep a clear connection with real problems, as epitomized by van de Ven's famous statement that: "there is nothing quite so practical as good theory" (van de Ven, 1989).

Encouragingly, there are many examples of close cooperation between OM researchers and practitioners that have led to seminal publications that have strongly influenced practice and further research as well as teaching. Consider concepts like total quality management (TQM), lean management, and quick response manufacturing, which developed in the business world long before they captured the attention of academics. The activity of engaged academic scholars was nevertheless instrumental to better understanding, theorizing, and generalizing these concepts beyond the contexts in which they were identified (e.g., Fisher *et al.*, 1994; Juran, 1994; Womack *et al.*, 2007) enabling their diffusion to a broader business audience. Remarkably, none of these seminal studies were published in academic journals. Instead, they were written as monographs and practitioner articles. Several hundred articles subsequently published by other scholars in academic journals have further developed and disseminated these concepts using a multitude of techniques including survey methods, lab experiments, secondary-data research, and analytical models (see, e.g., Cachon and Swinney, 2011; Croson and Donohue, 2006; Netland *et al.*, 2015; Shah and Ward, 2007; Staats *et al.*, 2011).

These examples prove the value of close cooperation between research and practice and benefits of engaged scholarship (van de Ven, 2007). Notwithstanding these powerful examples of the value created using this formidable mechanism for advancing knowledge, we find that OM as a discipline can do better at improving engagement with practice. The rapid and constantly changing nature of OM practice introduces significant and interesting opportunities for OM scholars to develop rigorous research tightly connected to practice. Noteworthy examples include the digitalization of operations networks and markets and implementation of socially and environmentally sustainable practices. Moreover, unexpected shocks like the COVID-19 pandemic and growing geo-political turmoil have also called into question established OM practices like global sourcing, prompting researchers to reexamine old questions, such as make versus buy decisions, in the light of new threats and opportunities. Yet engaged scholarship, despite repeated calls for more relevant business research, continues to be insufficiently practiced not only in our field (Tang, 2017) but in management generally (Spencer *et al.*, 2022). Although the concept of engaged scholarship is not new, we maintain that novel or overlooked methodologies like Intervention-Based Research, the focus of this monograph, are requisite to pursuing its adoption.

1.2 Engaged Scholarship Research

Engaged scholarship is a participative research approach to studying complex problems in social settings (van de Ven, 2007). Compared to traditional academic empirical research, engaged scholarship has three distinctive features. One, it starts from a real business problem, not from a theoretical conundrum that may or may not be relevant to practice. Two, in engaged scholarship produces theory that is informed by expertise of practitioner and other stakeholders, including

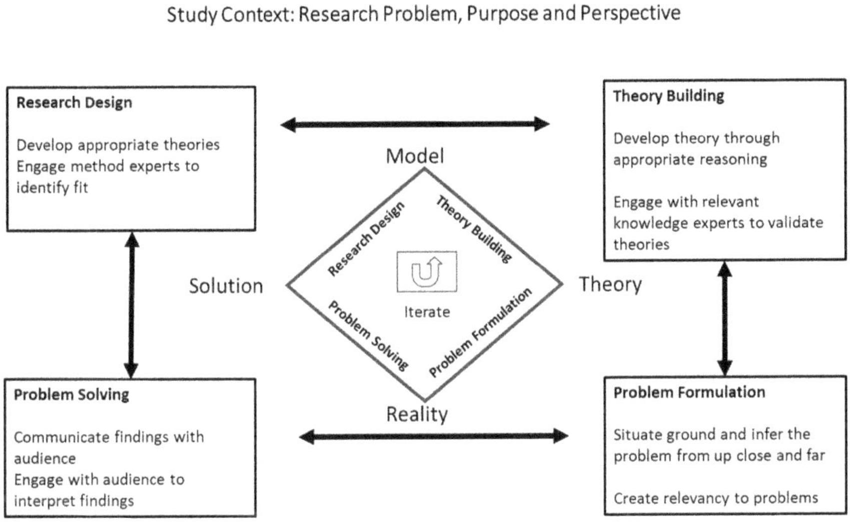

Figure 1.1: Engaged scholarship model for connecting research and practice. Adapted from van de Ven (2007).

researchers. Three, engaged scholarship follows a rigorous methodology that guides both the disciplined and rigorous search for solutions and interactions among the various stakeholders. Figure 1.1 illustrates the steps—problem formulation, theory building, research design, and problem solving—typically involved in engaged scholarship research.

This approach implies that our role as academic researchers studying business problems is to engage deeply with practitioners (from problem formulation to intervention evaluation), to co-produce relevant as well as scientifically valuable solutions. This engagement helps to ensure that researchers not only fully understand a problem, but also generate new theoretical insights. Engaged scholarship is not simply translating scientific into practical knowledge, but rather creating scientific and practical knowledge through learning communities that involve both researchers and practitioners (van de Ven and Johnson, 2006). Participation in such learning communities encourages researchers to solve not just one problem, but by remaining engaged discover and solve other problems. However, engaged scholarship maintains a clear separation between researcher and practitioner.

1.3 Intervention-Based Research: One Approach for Strengthening Engaged Scholarship

While engaged scholarship can be practiced using different methodologies, IBR offers a whole new level of researcher engagement with the problem to *develop novel theoretical* insights. The notion of "engaging with a problem" breaks with the tenet of natural science that dictates that scientists must not influence experimental outcomes and remain neutral and unbiased reporters of observed phenomena. With IBR, Social scientists to some extent forsake the aspired objectivity of natural science and, instead, actively interact with other stakeholders to more deeply understand and address a problem.

Active engagement with a problem with the goal of developing normative knowledge (Simon, 1988) is also employed in the Design Science method popular in the information systems discipline (van Aken, 2005). IBR, like Design Science, presumes researchers' deep engagement with both a problem and its organizational context, but the methods differ in purpose.

Design Science seeks to generate a design artifact or specific solution to a problem (a.k.a. "design proposition") that is of interest to an audience broader than its creators. In the information systems context, for example, a Design Science solution might be an algorithm or process model. The contributions of designed artifacts are intended to be pragmatic (i.e., solve a problem) rather than theoretical (i.e., expand or reformulate extant theory).

IBR, in contrast, leverages the researcher's involvement in tackling a problem first-hand to formulate new theoretical insights (Oliva, 2019). It generates knowledge that explains how problems can be solved through the formulation of causal models and provides insights related to the boundaries for applying these models. IBR is not incompatible with Design Science. A researcher engaged in IBR could also be involved in creating a designed artifact, the difference being that the description of said artifact is not the focus of IBR. With IBR, research attention shifts to reflecting on the experience to generate new theoretical insights including boundary conditions that improve the specificity of the theory. Although the know-how lessons are of interest to practitioners, what makes the experience potentially generalizable to other settings are updates to existing theory derived through abductive reasoning that explain unanticipated effects of the intervention. Insights generated by IBR are thus relevant and useful to both practicing managers and academicians (Reynes *et al.*, 2001).

A well-known illustration of the academic and practical merits of IBR is provided by the deep engagement of Marshall Fisher and Ananth Raman with fashion retailer *Sport Obermeyer* (Fisher, 1997; Fisher *et al.*, 1994) in which the authors looked at the chronic forecasting challenges of matching supply and demand. Through extensive field engagement, and using historical sales data, the authors developed and implemented a quick response-manufacturing strategy that both minimized stock-outs and markdown costs and yielded rich theoretical insights into the role of reduced lead times and small lot sizes in minimizing forecast errors. As well as benefiting the firm, the engagement produced a number of seminal research articles on reducing supply chain uncertainties.

The IBR approach promotes understanding of a problem not as "isolated parts" but as a "comprehensive whole" (Clark, 1989). By stepping outside of their own perspectives and actively engaging with relevant practitioners and other stakeholders, researchers, who may otherwise be prone to myopia and biases rooted in their disciplines and prior experiences, can achieve a more comprehensive understanding of the problem at hand. This, in effect, allows them to find the global optimum instead of getting stuck at a local maximum. The researchers who engaged with *Sport Obermeyer* on quick response manufacturing acknowledged that their development of improved heuristics that minimized overall inventory costs resulted from engagement with the managers that led to a number of assumptions underlying forecasting strategies being modified and enhanced (Fisher *et al.*, 1994). The foregoing example also illustrates how IBR can improve the relevance of business education by facilitating the creation of pedagogical materials immediately connected to real problems faced by organizations. The engagement with *Sport Obermeyer*, for example, yielded a seminal *Harvard Business Review* article (Fisher, 1997) as well as a teaching case (*Sport Obermeyer*) that continues to be widely used in MBA programs. Relevance for practice does *not*, however, imply immediate use. Years of further research and development are sometimes required before relevant research outcomes can be usefully applied. Consider, for instance, the series of studies by Chandrasekaran *et al.* (2016), Anand *et al.* (2021), and Chun *et al.* (2022) that investigated quality issues in a major hospital. Each of these studies further developed insights derived from earlier studies thereby cumulatively broadened our understanding on how to sustain quality practices in reducing patient readmissions.

IBR is, of course, not the only way to generate relevant and rigorous management research. Any methodology can in principle achieve the same goal. But only a handful of extremely talented scholars can ask themselves, as Coase (1937) did, "why do organizations exist?" and introduce the market versus hierarchy framework that has shaped research on make-versus-buy decisions for decades. IBR constitutes a valid methodological approach for ensuring an ongoing balance between rigor and relevance by fostering researchers' (i) continuous engagement with organizational actors on specific problems, and (ii) reflection on the theoretical underpinnings of those problems.

1.3.1 Positioning IBR within the Ecosystem of OM Research

To understand how it differs from other popular research approaches, it is necessary to place IBR within the context of the multiplicity of research strategies employed in OM. Figure 1.2 provides a framework for this comparison. The vertical axis represents the predominant method of reasoning, the horizontal axis the type of engagement, adopted by the researcher. Three modes of reasoning are common to social science research: deductive, inductive, and abductive. A researcher who develops a hypothesis based on existing theories and derives insights from subsequent testing using appropriate methods is employing deductive reasoning (Shadish *et al.*, 2001). Inductive reasoning generates insights and testable propositions from observations. Abductive reasoning, like inductive and deductive reasoning, begins with an observation. Unlike inductive reasoning, however, initial explanations do not thoroughly explain the problem, which generates an element of surprise that the researchers turn into a new theoretical explanation through iterative learning between the observation and theory (Mantere and Ketokivi,

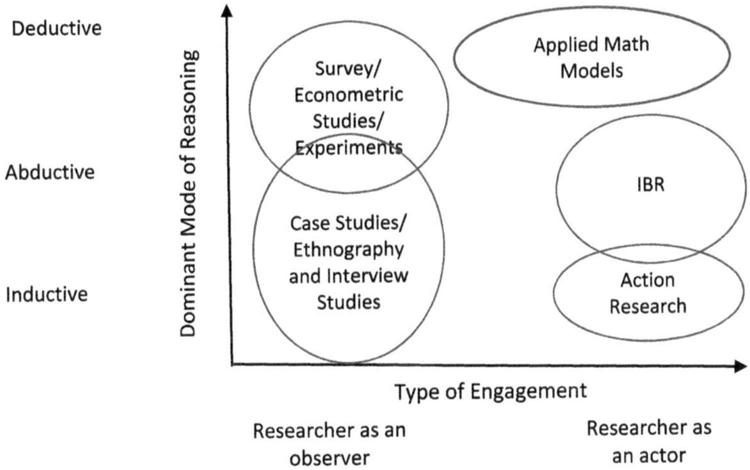

Figure 1.2: IBR in the OM research ecosystem.

2013). We are suggesting not that research studies employ only one mode of reasoning, but that OM research strategies may vary depending on the dominant mode of reasoning, plotted on the vertical axis with abductive positioned between deductive and inductive reasoning.

The horizontal axis plots the two modes of engagement described above, (i) the researcher as observer of the phenomenon of interest, and (ii) the researcher as active participant in the problem-solving process. OM researchers' traditional engagement with problems as observers reflects the former mode, in which a researcher gleans an understanding of its intricacies from frequent interaction with a problem (e.g., by developing case studies). The less commonly employed mode of pursuing a solution to a problem through active participation and collaboration with practitioners, by affording the researchers a deeper understanding of the problem and its complexity, can generate powerful insights. An overview of the different research methods employed in OM and how they compare in terms of these two dimensions is provided in Figure 1.2. As can be seen in the figure, the methods overlap. A researcher who adopts the abductive mode of reasoning, for instance, might employ both econometric and survey methods.

Figure 1.2 positions IBR across these three reasoning approaches inasmuch as researcher and practitioner co-create new knowledge by iterating between theory and data, the dominant mode of reasoning being abduction, which combines deduction and induction to generate new theoretical insights. IBR also involves active engagement by the researcher, an important distinction relative to methods like Grounded Theory Building, in which, the researcher is not supposed to shape or influence organizational phenomena.[2] Finally, it should be noted that there is a strong tradition of experimental field work based on testing the effects of interventions (e.g., process or organizational redesigns) on operational outcomes (Cook and Campbell, 1979; Shadish *et al.*, 2001). Although the experimental treatment in those studies it is often an intervention, we do not include them explicitly in this study as once the treatment is designed, the researcher is expected to become an objective observer of the intervention's effectiveness as opposed to an enable or facilitator of the change process.

Although all forms are important to OM research, a significant deficit is observed in active researcher involvement in the problem-solving process. Indeed, active engagement by the researcher is sometimes frowned upon by academics of the opinion that it might influence the study design. Yet one of the attributes of active engagement is its capacity to simultaneously exert an immediate impact on practice and contribute to the generation of new theoretical insights.

1.3.2 Issues in Linking the Worlds of Practice and Research

Academics and practitioners have undeniably different goals and focuses of interest. Practitioners tend to be interested primarily in context-specific issues (and less in the generalizability of their problems) and to be rewarded for dealing with these issues to the extent that doing so serves the organization's objectives. Researchers' interest extends beyond problem-solving that has an impact to generalizing their findings, which serves their theoretical interests, pedagogical mission as well as academic careers (Gulati, 2007). The result is that researchers seeking broad

[2] In Figure 1.2, we situate action research (AR) across the abductive and inductive modes of reasoning. Although we argue in Section 2 that it is one of the research models of IBR, AR is often used to structure interventions that do not necessarily drive the reflection that yields theoretical developments. See, for example, Nair *et al.* (2011).

theoretical problems to solve often struggle to capture the attention and engagement of the practitioner community (van de Ven and Johnson, 2006).

IBR strikes a happy medium wherein researchers generate new insights of interest to other academics at the same time that they contribute to the practitioner community by solving real problems. It is important, however, to note two major caveats related to using IBR. The first one relates to the fact that IBR is just another research method and should follow the research question. That is, not all problems can be solved using an IBR. We discuss in Section 2 when and how to use IBR to address OM problems. The other caveat is that IBR, like all research strategies, entails a set of risks that must be weighed by the researcher. Typical risks and possible mitigation strategies are considered in Section 3. A thorough exploration of these risks with their advisors is recommended for PhD students interested in employing IBR.

1.4 Main Objective of this Monograph

This monograph describes the purpose and necessity of IBR in Operations Management. In Section 2, we illustrate how OM researchers can learn from interventions. We investigate specifically the role of abductive reasoning and how it takes shape during an IBR project. We also discuss how IBR can be employed to develop process theories; a concept mostly ignored in the OM research. Section 3 elaborates on the process of conducting IBR and challenges associated with this research strategy as well as the tools and skillsets needed by researchers who would adopt this method. Examples from OM research of IBR used in various contexts including healthcare delivery, manufacturing, and services are provided in Section 4, in which we also discuss how to extract theoretical and practical insights from interventions. We conclude by emphasizing the importance of adding this line of enquiry to OM research and call for more work using this method. We hope that the Operations Management community will find this monograph to be a useful guide for identifying research problems suited to IBR and applying this method to generate new knowledge in exciting new areas of research.

2

How to Learn from Interventions

The previous section introduced intervention-based research as a different approach to developing valid theory with the potential to have an impact on business practice and performance. IBR confronts a theory with the vicissitudes of real-world implementation and uses it to influence a real-world situation in an empirically relevant way that goes beyond data collection or hypotheses testing. The attempt to *apply* a theory, if properly structured, can reveal new insights into how it could be improved by either expanding the scope of generalization or defining the specificity of the range of instances in which it applies. This section emphasizes how intervention generates opportunities to improve theories and what is needed to effectively leverage the experience. We define more precisely the types of insights that might be gained from intervention and explain how the validity of inferred insights can be substantiated by the design and documentation of interventions. The preceding section answered the questions "*Why IBR?*" This section answers, from an epistemological perspective, the questions "*What kind of knowledge does IBR generate?*" and "*What needs to happen for IBR to work?*" as a prelude to taking up in Section 3 the matter of how to conduct IBR.

We present abductive reasoning as the epistemological foundation of IBR and a complement to the inductive and deductive reasoning that dominate the way scientific research is reported (Section 2.1). We also describe two modes of IBR that explicitly leverage intervention to yield interesting, that is, unexpected outcomes, that fuel the development of theoretical insights (Section 2.2). We then expand on the attributes and generalizability of good hypotheses operationalized from theories that emerge from the abductive process (Section 2.3). Finally, we examine the implications of this epistemological structure for the selection of promising interventions and standards of evidence to support the proposed theoretical insights (Section 2.4).

2.1 Abductive Reasoning

In using a theory to confront real-world problem situations, IBR is likely to generate mismatches between theoretical expectations and actual outcomes of interventions. The theorizing process required to explain new observed outcomes is best described as *abductive reasoning*, described by Peirce (1955) as a reasoning strategy that seeks the simplest, most likely explanation for a new set of empirical observations. Also called "retroduction" (Hanson, 1958; Peirce, 1955), abductive reasoning complements deductive and inductive reasoning in formal logic (Peirce, 1965). An abductive argument states that it is implausible that the premises are true and conclusions false (Hurley, 2000), and unlike induction, which is based on observed empirical regularities, is based on reasoning. Although Peirce suggests that deduction is the strongest and abduction the weakest form of argument, the latter is nevertheless an essential element of the scientific enterprise because it connects unexplained empirical facts to theoretical ideas.

The deductive approach to research design is the traditional hypotheses testing strategy, which requires the development of predictions from an existing theory (hypotheses) and the design of an experiment to generate data to determine how closely observations match the theory. If the experimental outcome matches the predictions from theory, we fail to falsify and, through induction, find (weak) support for the hypothesis; no experimental outcome will ever *confirm* a hypothesis

(Oreskes *et al.*, 1994).[1] If the outcome is not as expected and the experimental design deemed valid and reliable, it is necessary to modify the theory to account for the discrepant observations.[2] The articulation of a theory or hypothesis that explains the data is what Peirce referred to as abduction (Peirce, 1965, 5.145, EP 2:205), and it differs from induction in that in abduction "the process of forming an explanatory hypothesis ... introduces a new idea" (Peirce, 1965, 5.171, EO 2:216), whereas induction only determines how well the consequences deduced from a hypotheses accord with the facts (Mcauliffe, 2015).

Note that non-conforming experimental outcomes are not the only source of new hypotheses, as new observations not accounted for by existing theories can also prompt the abductive process to generate plausible explanations. Because plausible new theories or hypotheses, regardless of their source, need to be verified or tested with a different sample using a deductive research approach, most research programs iterate between research strategies in which deductive studies generate questions or unexpected data that lead to abductive theory development, and abductive reasoning that generates theories that stimulate deductive research (Hanson, 1958; Poole *et al.*, 2000; Rozeboom, 1997). Consider, by way of an example, a research project in which one of the authors was involved. Oliva and Kallenberg (2003) found, using semi-structured interviews and detailed archival assessment of eleven German equipment manufacturers' experience integrating services with their products (the so-called servitization strategy), that organizations that managed to successfully bundle services with their products had created separate services organizations within the firm. At the time, the authors hypothesized, abductively, that the creation of separate business units protected the personnel responsible for delivering the

[1]This hypothesis-testing period is part of what Kuhn (1970) calls "normal science."

[2]It is in practice difficult to reject a hypothesis, as researchers will often protect core hypotheses by questioning the experimental design and execution or modifying background/auxiliary assumptions that might be wrong. The process of protecting core hypotheses is termed the Quine-Duhem thesis (Cook and Campbell, 1979). According to Kuhn (1970), adoption of a new core hypothesis only occurs when it is capable or resolving anomalies accumulated during the normal science period.

services from the throughput and efficiency goals common in manufacturing organizations, which tend to erode service quality (Oliva, 2001; Oliva and Sterman, 2001). A large-sample study (Oliva *et al.*, 2012) was later designed, using a deductive research strategy, to explore the mediation effect of the degree of separation of service business units on the relationship between managerial commitment to a service strategy and service business performance. Although from a non-IBR project, this example illustrates the process of theory development as iteration between the creative stage of generating plausible hypotheses (the abduction process) and the deductive research design by which the hypotheses are tested.

Because it is designed to help an organization achieve a transformational goal based on some foundational theory, an intervention cannot be considered a traditional deductive research design for purposes of testing the theory, as, by design, it has a strong confirmation bias. That an intervention has a well-announced purpose and motivation makes it infeasible for a researcher to disentangle the possibility that agents in a problem situation might modify their behavior to refute or conform to a preconceived theory (Oliva, 2019). Thus, an intervention, if executed correctly, could at best be used to generate or collect new observations about a particular phenomenon, and, if sought, can abductively generate propositions or theories to best explain that data. As such, the documentation standards for an IBR project should allow the researchers to code the observations in a way that they can be tested and questioned for the generation of the new propositions. It being impossible to anticipate what will be novel about intervention outcomes, the coding of data for further analysis poses a major challenge. More varied and detailed data will, of course, support the generation of more accurate and precise propositions. Strategies and techniques for data gathering and documentation are explored in the following section. We consider below two important modes in which an intervention can generate surprising data that requires new explanations.

2.2 Generating Surprises Through IBR[3]

An intervention involves an iterative process of identifying a problem, planning, acting, and evaluating (Argyris *et al.*, 1985; Deming, 1982). This generic intervention process implies a clearly stated methodology, a prediction of the outcome of the intervention, and an assessment of the effectiveness of the theory used to design the intervention. There cannot be an intervention without an explicit normative theory that, given a statement of assumptions and intentions, suggests a certain course of action (Schein, 1987). Checkland (1985) proposes that an intervention is guided by a deliberate strategy or methodology (M) that makes use of a theoretical framework (T) to improve a situation (S), where the methodology provides specific guidelines for "how" the theoretical framework will be used to improve the problem situation. Thus, an intervention in which the methodology is explicitly stated, documented, and reflected upon has the potential to generate mismatches between intentions and assumptions and what happens when the methodology is put into practice, that is, insights about T, S, or M (see Figure 2.1). Such mismatches (i.e., surprising outcomes) generate opportunities to update and correct understanding of a problem situation and the models or theories used to intervene in it. That is, an intervention might reveal shortcomings that impede, or suggest improvements needed to facilitate, a theory's ability to explain the results obtained. Of course, surprising outcomes can also emerge from a better understanding of a problem situation (S) or gaps revealed in methodological guidelines (M) (see the discussion in Oliva, 2019 § 2.1). Such opportunities for learning, though they might contribute to an intervention's eventual success, do not, however, inform theory development. Oliva (2019) refers to the use of intervention to empirically test the usefulness and applicability of existing theory as Mode 1 of IBR.

Note that the research design of Mode 1 IBR is not so different from deductive research design in that deduction is employed to design an intervention based on predictions derived from theory. The difference is that, unlike an experiment, which is designed to falsify

[3]The arguments presented in this subsection were originally developed, in greater detail, in Oliva (2019).

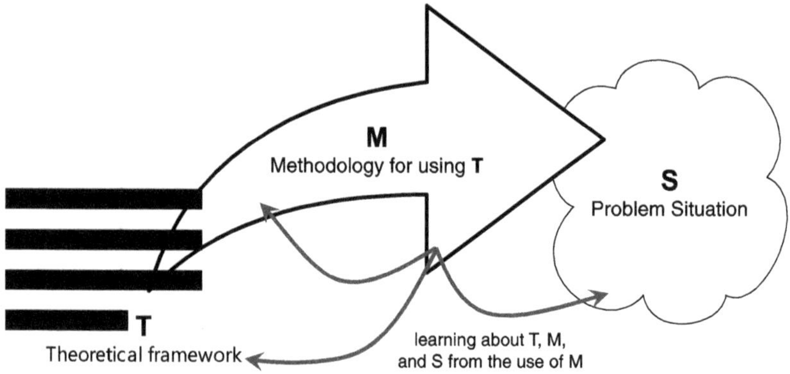

Figure 2.1: Learning from interventions. Adapted from Checkland (1985).

the null hypothesis while controlling for other factors, an intervention is designed to *confirm* a theory and, as discussed above, executed by and upon human actors capable of modifying their behavior once the purpose of the intervention is revealed. Moreover, a practitioner might adjust an intervention methodology in response to novel information or unanticipated responses from the actors in a problem situation. This renders the intervenor no longer (as expected during the execution of an experiment) an objective observer of the results obtained by the application of the theory. Engagement with the situation (see Engaged Scholarship Research in the previous section) creates an opportunity to learn from practitioners' experience, but renders the intervention process a *biased* effort to achieve success with the theory and obtain expected outcomes. An intervention thus neither constitutes a formal test of theory nor possesses the informative power of an experiment. In Mode 1 IBR, the potential to generate new insights is predicated on how well methodological assumptions and expectations (i.e., the normative theory guiding the intervention) are stated *a priori*.

Whereas Mode 1 IBR employs surprise outcomes (vis-à-vis the theoretical expectations) to revise the theory guiding an intervention, Mode 2 IBR (Oliva, 2019), although it also leverages the fact that an intervention has clear expectations of the end-state, is concerned with identifying *how* the intervention process occasioned those outcomes. A well-designed and executed intervention implies, as noted above,

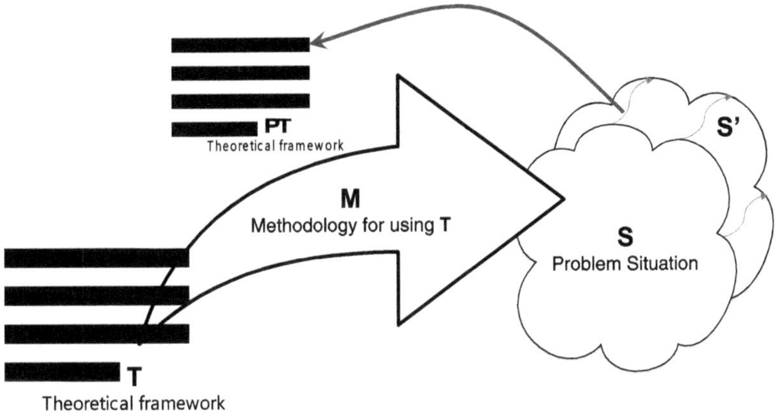

Figure 2.2: Learning form the outcomes of an intervention – Process Theory. Adapted from Oliva (2019).

deliberate planning and deployment of resources. If, despite these efforts and resources, the target transformation is not achieved, the documented intervention constitutes a rich and unique set of evidence with which to explore the questions, "How did we get there?" and "Why did we get there?" (see Figure 2.2). In this research mode, unexpected changes resulting from an intervention (the transition from an initial condition S to an endpoint S') are considered the phenomenon that needs to be further explained.

To explain *how* an intervention is responsible for an observed outcome, it is necessary to elucidate the *trajectory* that the problem situation followed from its initial state to the surprising end state, which shifts the theoretical focus from variance to process theories (Mohr, 1982; Monge, 1990). Process theories identify how entities engage and are affected by events and provide time dependent explanations of how and why things happen. Thus, to make sense of the trajectory of a problem situation, it is necessary to account for the sequence of actions and events that characterize an intervention. Though process theories have a clear standing in the natural sciences (e.g., theory of evolution), they are less frequently invoked in the social sciences. This is perhaps due to the fact that social scientists are not normally trained in the development and testing of process theories (Oliva, 2019) and the expected difficulties in publishing this non-traditional work. Recent methodological developments (see Oliva, 2019 § 3.1, for an overview) and calls for more use of process theories across disciplines (e.g., Langley *et al.*, 2013; Monge, 1990; Poole *et al.*, 2000; Sterman *et al.*, 2015) seem to be removing these obstacles.

Theorizing from process data presents unique challenges. Process data, because of its temporal embeddedness, often lacks consistency of measurement over time and captures sequences of events at multiple levels (units of analysis) and across a variety of dimensions (e.g., changing relationships, feelings, or interpretations) (Langley, 1999; Poole *et al.*, 2000). Strategies for making sense of this type of data are varied, and cover the spectrum from articulation of narratives (e.g., Pentland, 1999) to computer simulation (e.g., Cyert and March, 1963; Forrester, 1961), Langley (1999) and Poole *et al.* (2000) being among those who offer strategies and techniques for dealing with process data. In any case, the theorizing process requires going beyond describing what happened to explaining why events unfolded the way they did.

In Mode 2 IBR, when the results obtained from the theory (T) used to design an intervention are unexpected, a new theory (PT in Figure 2.2) is needed to explain them, resulting in theorizing that likely generates a new set of propositions and theories rather than the incremental improvement that occurs in Mode 1 IBR. Despite differences in methods and theorizing process, the potential to generate new insights is, for Mode 1 and Mode 2 IBR alike, predicated on how well methodological assumptions and expectations are stated *before* the intervention.

2.3 Theoretical Insights from IBR

The outcomes of an intervention are contingent on the specifics of the situation being addressed, the capabilities of the team deploying the intervention, and the theories guiding the intervention process. If the goal is to have future successful interventions, it is desirable to capture the methodological insights of successful interventions. This is equivalent to capturing the *design propositions* argued for by Design Science (Denyer *et al.*, 2008; van Aken *et al.*, 2016) and would be in line with the goals of a practitioner or a consultant. The goal, from this perspective, is to document the intervention in sufficient detail to ensure its replicability, so-called pragmatic validity (van Aken *et al.*, 2016). If, however, the goal is to modify or update existing theory as a result of the intervention, it is important to recognize the types of theoretical improvements that can be made with IBR and the desirable attributes of the theoretical propositions.

Theories, "ordered set[s] of assertions about a generic behavior or structure assumed to hold throughout a significant range of specific instances" (Sutherland, 1975, p. 9), are never finished products and always in a state of development (Mohr, 1982, p. 6; Runkel and Runkel, 1984, pp. 129–130; Weick, 1989, p. 516). Not only is it not possible to verify a hypothesis (Oreskes *et al.*, 1994), but existing theories can always be improved by expanding the **scope of their assertions** or the specificity of the **range of instances** to which they apply (Weick, 1989, p. 516). We explore the advantages and potential contribution of IBR in each of these expansion strategies.

In terms of **scope of assertions**, that is, how generic is the focus of the theoretical constructs, the potential of IBR, by nature of the intervention process, is high. Interventions are always situation-specific, that is, they are a *particular* instance of the application of a theory in a specific context. Insights from an intervention will thus likely expand the scope of assertions by providing evidence of constructs more precise than those in the general theory used to design the intervention. The logic of the abduction process dictates the standard of evidence needed to generate the hypothesis that best explains surprising data from an intervention, whether detected under Mode 1 or Mode 2. As for desired attributes of proposed hypotheses, there are two. Proposed explanations need to be *accurate*, that is, their description should correspond to the real-world situation such that actors in the situation would recognize the description (Forrester, 1961, p. 57), and be fully grounded in all available data (Strauss and Corbin, 1990). The researcher being intimately involved in the intervention, IBR can be expected to positively affect the accuracy of abductively generated hypotheses. The other desired attribute is that causal statements be *precise*, that is, sharply defined, specific, and "not-vague" (Forrester, 1961, p. 57), thereby providing a refutable description with "multiple points of testing" (Bell and Bell, 1980; Bell and Senge, 1980; Oliva, 2003). IBR affords researchers an opportunity to add precision to any novel insights generated. Thus, at a minimum, proposed hypotheses need to explain, accurately and precisely, anomalous data; the *raison d'etre* of new propositions generated by abductive logic. Propositions that emerge from an abductive process to the extent that they are more accurate and precise than the theory used to guide an intervention, will constitute potential improvements, contingent on being tested, to the "set of assertions about a generic behavior" captured by the theory. What we are saying is not that IBR infallibly improves the accuracy and precision of emerging theories, but that it can confer certain advantages on the abductive process.

Consider, by way of example, the process theory developed by Oliva (2019) to explain the exponential reduction of triggered audits to correct inventory record inaccuracies. Oliva first presented the data accurately and precisely, reporting the number of audits triggered per week and confirming, via regression, that the audits followed an exponential decay. He then articulated why this result was surprising, observing that although exponential decay of failures has been found in improvement programs that addressed root causes (Schneiderman, 1988), this was not expected in situations in which the intervention addressed only problem symptoms. In this case, the audits corrected inventory inaccuracies, but did nothing to address the underlying operational issues that caused the inaccuracies. This surprising result triggered the abduction process that resulted in a process theory that provided an endogenous feedback explanation, based on stocks and flows, for the observed decay. The theory was articulated in a formal model that provided a precise explanation (conditions, relative strengths of feedback mechanisms) and ensured logical consistency (e.g., unit consistency). Furthermore, the model was grounded in previous knowledge (i.e., well understood causal terms) and provides multiple points for testing the dynamic hypotheses, thus making the theory empirically testable.

Regarding the **range of instances** to which theoretical insights apply, that is, the external validity of developed claims, it should be noted that intervention-based insights, like the insights from case studies, are intended to generalize to theory as opposed to a population

(Oliva, 2019). The intervention is not a "sample" in the common statistical sense, but rather a rich base from which to develop generalizable theoretical insights. Yin (2003b, p. 10) calls this generalizing process *analytic generalization* as opposed to the *statistical generalization* associated with sampling studies, and Meredith (1998, p. 450) refers to it as *theoretic generalizability* as opposed to the *assumptive generalizability* epitomized in mathematical modeling research. That is, the transferability of insights to other settings will depend on the extent that theoretical assumptions apply to settings rather than some general population characteristic. In their study of the sales and operations planning (S&OP) process, for example, Oliva and Watson (2011), "by characterizing the supply chain planning context as exhibiting functional differentiation and [their site's] planning approach as being complicated by functional mistrust and poor inter-temporal coordination," generalize their insights to a range of planning dysfunctions that, although not identical to the ones found at the research site, emerge from similar causes. Similarly, Chuang *et al.* (2021) distill the challenges faced by their research site's forecasting organization to a set of characteristics (e.g., supply chain coordination for innovative, short product life, markets in which the supplier does not have access to detailed material requirements) that not only explain observed difficulties in the problem situation, but also define the scope of theoretical generalization justified by the evidence.

Whether theoretical improvement is through expansion of the *scope* of claims or *range* of application of insights, the abduction process, and entire epistemological structure described above for IBR, does *not* constitute a test of theory. The exercise being the generation of a new set of hypotheses based on freshly obtained data from an intervention, the outcome of the IBR process needs to be testable statements of causality, that is, propositions that could in essence be falsified through experimental testing or conceivable observations (Oliva, 2020).

Intervention being an attempt to deploy a particular theory to modify the real world, the process is bound to generate interesting (unexpected or surprising) data. This affords an opportunity to generate, by engaging in an abductive process, new hypotheses or conjectures that propel the development or updating of existing theory. Such conjectures should, at a minimum, explain accurately and precisely observed anomalous data, and their quality be judged in the manner of any other refutable scientific hypotheses: are they logically sound, consistent with existing knowledge, and empirically testable? (Bunge, 1967)[4]

2.4 Implications for Research Selection/Design and Reporting

IBR was characterized in Section 1 as researchers engaged in problem situations to develop novel theoretical insights. In this section, we have learned that to be useful *for theoretical development*, an intervention must yield interesting or unexpected outcomes (Mode 1) or endpoints (Mode 2), and that these outcomes, and the processes that render them, need to be documented in a way that enables a methodologically sound and theoretically innovative abductive process.

Note that "theoretical developments" are a different dimension for assessing interventions and not necessarily in line with the intended practical outcomes of the intervention. That is to say, an intervention can be successful in achieving intended outcomes and not yield surprises that warrant further theorizing. Alternatively, poor outcomes from an intervention might open a new theorizing space in which to pursue an explanation for the failure. Interesting data may, of course, be generated by nuanced changes in an intervention strategy or surprisingly good outcomes that nevertheless invite further reflection.

So, given the above distinctions, what are the characteristics of situations in which IBR might be a promising strategy? Surprising or unexpected results are more likely to emerge from ill-structured situations, variously labeled messy (Ackoff, 1981), complex, swampy (Schön, 1987), and wicked (Churchman, 1967; Rittel and Webbet, 1973), and characterized by ill-defined interactions among operational, financial, social, and political factors and lack of agreement on problem definition and identification of root causes owing to the presence of

[4]These criteria, collectively, are equivalent to the conditions Peirce identified as necessary for a hypothesis worthiness of consideration, i.e., the hypotheses should explain the facts in question and should be experimentally verifiable (Mcauliffe, 2015, p. 303). Peirce also listed three economic considerations for the selection of hypotheses: how expensive is to test the hypotheses, how likely is the hypotheses to be true, and how preferable is this line of inquire relative to alternatives (see Mcauliffe, 2015, for details on these economic considerations).

multiple stakeholders. A successful strategy in such situations is to reframe the problem in such a way that it is possible to identify improvement initiatives that are systemically desirable and culturally feasible (Checkland, 1981). Insights from such reframing will usually generate interesting theoretical developments. Ill-structured situations are promising because they necessitate interventions dealing with uncertainty and unknowns and making sense of which, at least in one context, can be a fruitful source of theoretical insights. Akkermans *et al.* (2019), for example, discovered when attempting to develop new contracts for service providers in a complex telecommunications firm that traditional performance indicators that do not consider the fact that services are often coproduced failed to successfully coordinate partners. This realization led the researchers to reframe the problem and create a new type of performance-based contract.

If IBR's potential in wicked problem situations derives from uncertainty surrounding problem definition, a complementary strategy would be to look for situations in which the source of uncertainty is the theory being employed to design an intervention. Situations in which the driving theory or technology is not mature (Edmondson and McManus, 2007), or in which a well-understood theory is being used to intervene in a new context, also offer promising pastures for IBR. An example of the former is Chuang *et al.* (2021), who used machine learning to improve forecasts for volatile demand patterns, of the latter, Chun *et al.* (2022), who used Donabedian's process of care theory (Donabedian, 1988) to understand post-surgical transitions.

Given that the success of IBR is predicated on the ability to abductively generate explanations for observed results and demonstrate how revisions to theory address surprising operational outcomes, what are the documentation requirements for IBR? A description of the methods employed in an intervention as well as documentation of the results should provide evidence sufficient to judge the appropriateness of abductive inferences. The standard is similar to that for case study research (Yin, 2003a, 2003b), in which the goal is to present relevant evidence to support the claims rather than all the qualitative data gathered.

If the contribution of IBR is the generation of new propositions (conjectures or hypotheses), *what matters in writing an IBR piece is the theorizing process and quality of the propositions that emerge from it.* The goal of the authors should be, as in a case study, to convince the reader that (a) the observed data require new explanations, and (b) that the proposed explanations can explain the observed data, and (c) that these explanations are worth pursuing through further testing (i.e., they are logically sound, congruent with current knowledge, and empirically testable). An intervention is needed to generate data, but its details are relevant only if they inform the theorizing process. Because the difficulty of designing and executing an intervention makes it tempting to report all its details, it is important to remember that an intervention is only the data generating process. Once a process and the anomalies it creates are described, the substantive part of an IBR contribution is the description of the theorizing process and assessment of the quality of the proposed explanations by the criteria defined above. The next section presents techniques and strategies for facilitating the documentation of evidence and the reflection requisite to the theory generating process.

3

Conducting Intervention-Based Research

The need for greater engagement with practice is a common theme among management scholars. Herbert Simon, Henry Mintzberg, Andrew van de Ven, and countless other prominent researchers have long advocated the importance of engaging with practice and practitioners to produce more relevant research. There is likely no simple, or single, answer as to why so few scholars heed this admonition. The overall academic ecosystem is inward looking, careers being made based on academic publication and not impact on business practice. The risky enterprise of engaged scholarship is left out of the plans of academics inclined to remain in their comfort zone. Doctoral programs consequently emphasize understanding of the literature and its theoretical conundrums at the expense of understanding real problems in organizations and society. Overcoming these issues and embracing Intervention-Based Research presents the scholar with unique challenges, which we have come to realize through years of experience and countless interactions with businesspeople at all levels. Our purpose in this section is to provide an overview of and suggest possible remedies to what we have identified as significant challenges to IBR. The advice offered reflects personal experience conducting and reporting IBR as well as lessons learned from successes and failures. This overview, albeit neither complete nor universally valid, constitutes a preliminary checklist of things to at least consider when attempting to design and execute IBR, as well as validate its findings.

3.1 Creating an IBR Opportunity

Any young scholar willing to employ IBR cannot escape the fundamental question of how to identify IBR opportunities. Useful sources of contacts for IBR include executive training, university events that target practitioners, centers active within these organizations as well as personal contacts. These channels are, however, only starting points. To turn a LinkedIn message from an alumnus into a project entails effort and skill, as well as an overarching understanding the potential roadblock to success.

A general recommendation before investing too much in any attempt to shape an IBR opportunity is to make sure that your contact has the power to make the project happen. Enthusiasm is not sufficient if this person has no real decision-making authority on the area where you want to focus on. In this case, you need to see whether a higher-ranking manager can be brought onboard or if, instead, you would better not pursue the opportunity further. Assuming you reach the "right" decision maker, we present in Figure 3.1 four guidelines for generating IBR opportunities.

3.1.1 Practice Empathy

Jump-starting collaboration between a university researcher and practitioner is a delicate process that requires mutual understanding. Businesspeople by and large are not accustomed to thinking of management research as a valuable activity, at least not initially. They understand that engineering and biomedical research can generate useful processes or products, but what is the output of management research? What kind of problems can it solve or inform? Researchers who set out on the bumpy road towards IBR must first listen to their prospective business counterparts and try to understand the problems and issues they face.

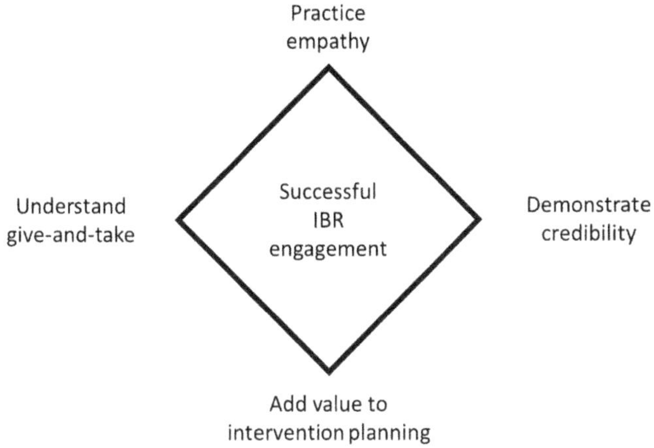

Figure 3.1: Factors that drive successful IBR engagements.

Businesspeople are too familiar with scholars "just looking for data" or who push their research agenda without regard for the genuine business concerns of the site originating the data. The way to capture the attention of businesspeople is to connect with the issues with which they are occupied or preoccupied. This is the sense in which researchers inclined to pursue IBR must be emphatic. Being emphatic does not mean being willing to study anything of concern to a businessperson. What it does entail is communicating a genuine interest in understanding the views or concerns of prospective business counterparts, in the absence of which researchers fail to build trust, a key enabler of collaboration. In practice, this means that empathy is more than an attitude. It must be reflected in researchers' willingness to adapt, within the context of the overall research program, the focus of the study to a real problem at hand.

One of the authors recalls an instance of two young professors who, invited to talk to a prospective sponsor of an innovation center, relentlessly attempted to steer the conversation towards their respective research agendas. Realizing that they viewed the center merely as a vehicle for supporting their chosen lines of research, the prospective sponsor withdrew from the conversation. A more productive outcome was realized from an invitation to one of the authors to participate in a conversation about a broad healthcare issue. Acquainted through the conversation with low hanging fruit that might benefit the organization (i.e., a training program), the author elected to cultivate respect and trust before pursuing further engagement opportunities by offering to provide the desired training pro-bono.

3.1.2 Understand "Give and Take"

Once a common area of interest has been identified, the "what can you do for me" question becomes central to the researcher-business counterpart conversation. Establishing the capability to deliver on a firm's expectations constitutes the second stage of the trust building process. Although not always an option, following the consulting practice of showcasing the results or benefits of previous IBR studies can help to establish credibility. This, of course, puts researchers starting a new line of research or lacking prior IBR or even field study experience at a disadvantage.

A researcher can sometimes overcome a deficit of experience by demonstrating expertise in exploiting available secondary, non-experimental data to analyze questions of interest to the business counterpart, but not necessarily of academia. Consider for instance this illustrative situation. One of the authors was interested in engaging with a high-tech firm to explore how project control data could be used to improve project management practices. The company was willing to engage in data analytics, but they were reluctant to delimit the scope of the collaboration to an IBR initiative that they deemed as relatively risky and narrow. The research team hence agreed to quantify via regression the outcomes of project planning practices that were firmly established in the literature (that is, not of interest for an academic publication). In this way the firm secured a useful input, while the research team did not waste the effort, as in this way they got a sense of possible research opportunities that resonated with the burning issues of the firm, securing the basis for a successful collaboration and scientific output (see Momcheva *et al.*, 2022).

Another means, alluded to above, of conveying the potential value of initiating an IBR project in the absence of prior experience is to offer employees at the target site free training on a topic not directly related to the research. One of the authors, as a way to pursue access to real problems and data, built rapport with key decision makers by teaching, at no charge, a course on value stream mapping. Another made a presentation on a contemporary topic (i.e., data ethics) to senior leaders at a large auto manufacturer before engaging them in conversation about a research agenda.

A researcher with a proven track record in IBR related to the topic of interest can reasonably and fairly charge a business counterpart for costs incurred (e.g., supporting doctoral and post-doctoral students, but also faculty fees, etc.). Charging for a research "service" is also a means of communicating its value and verifying the interest of the business counterpart. Institutional factors and agreements between business partners' and researchers' organizations will play a role in determining appropriate compensation.

3.1.3 Demonstrate Credibility

The next level in persuading a business counterpart that the researcher can execute what he or she promises, is to leverage data from interventions that the target site executed before the current engagement. This is not per se IBR, because the researcher was not actually involved in the intervention but serves a purpose in the engagement process. In fact, a key problem for practitioners is that they struggle to imagine what the researcher will do and how the outcome will look like. Doing an ex-post evaluation of an intervention previously executed would take away a lot of uncertainty in terms of what the researcher can do. Of course, if what you can do does not make much sense for practice, this step would kill your project! On the other hand, by engaging in this exercise the researcher would realize possible deficiencies in extant data collection procedures or scope within the target organization. This would enable a better design of the data collection apparatus associated to the target intervention.

A further reason for pursuing ex-post evaluations of previous interventions is that, should interesting results be discovered, a study can become, per se, a publishable field experiment. Papers reporting ex-post studies of field experiments conducted without the involvement of the author are not unusual and, for experiments that were well designed, can be quite useful.

3.1.4 Add Value to Intervention Planning

Business partners buy-in to an IBR project is most effectively secured by demonstrating a researcher's ability to help with an intervention's design. We cannot forget that businesspeople are used to collaborating with external consultants, which provide detailed sequences of activities and timetables in their project plans. Yet, the more exploratory nature of IBR compared to consulting makes designing an intervention not that easy. It requires deep knowledge of the setting in which it is to be executed, an understanding of what data can realistically be collected, a plan for executing the intervention, and an appreciation for how likely is to be accepted or opposed by relevant stakeholders. One main way for researcher to address this demanding requirement is to focus on a specific industry or problem type. Experience would spill over from one project to another, hence increasing the mastery in the design of interventions.

For example, one of the authors has studied application services (e.g., software maintenance) for quite a few years (Bonet and Salvador, 2017; Madiedo *et al.*, 2020; Salvador *et al.*, 2021). He learned that typically the ticketing system used to route tasks to workers tracks times, types of tasks, workers executing the task etc. So, once he got the opportunity of designing an intervention to create a Machine Learning algorithm for task completion estimation in a similar setting, he already knew which important predictors were likely to be available and which not. Based on previous analyses in different sites, he had an estimate of what effort would be needed for the project, and what level of accuracy was to be expected from the ML predictions.

Business counterparts' interest in engagement sometimes extends beyond solving a practical problem to publishing research in their own field. For instance, in healthcare physicians and nurses are quite interested in seeing the fruits of research in which they are participants published in medical journals. They are not necessarily interested in publication in business journals though. Attention to the specifics of contracts and publication venues (e.g., trade journals, training manuals) can result in a win-win engagement for researchers and their business counterparts alike. Research questions and data will necessarily differ between publishing venues. One of the authors, before setting up an intervention to investigate readmission issues after major transplant surgery, drafted a manuscript that attracted more interest from the medical research community than from management scholars (Chandrasekaran *et al.*, 2016), but the intervention subsequently yielded more management oriented papers (Anand *et al.*, 2021; Chandrasekaran and Toussaint, 2019; Chun *et al.*, 2022). It is important to understand the duality of publication objectives in IBR projects.

The implicit lesson here is that it is incumbent on researchers who choose to pursue IBR to develop specialized knowledge about a particular industry or cross-industry problem as well as of the aims and objectives of industry partners. Generalists are likely to struggle to connect with managers and sell the idea of partnering in IBR-type studies.

3.2 Mind the Killers of Successful of IBR Execution

You think you've made it. Your business counterpart has signed on to execute the study under discussion. But if you think the worst is over, think again. Myriad factors that can hinder the successful execution of a project must be considered in the drafting of a final contract as well as in a project's execution. We review below some of the factors that can impede the successful execution of IBR (see Figure 3.2).

3.2.1 Key Contact(s) Overload

Even if they're favorably disposed to a project, the people with spending authority to sponsor it out of some corporate budget are likely to be quite busy and unlikely to be able to support the project day-to-day. It is essential to identify at the outset a key contact at the operational level. This is the person who will provide the support needed to get things done as well as to secure, when necessary, the attention and a slot in the agenda of the top-level sponsor. It is well to keep in mind that

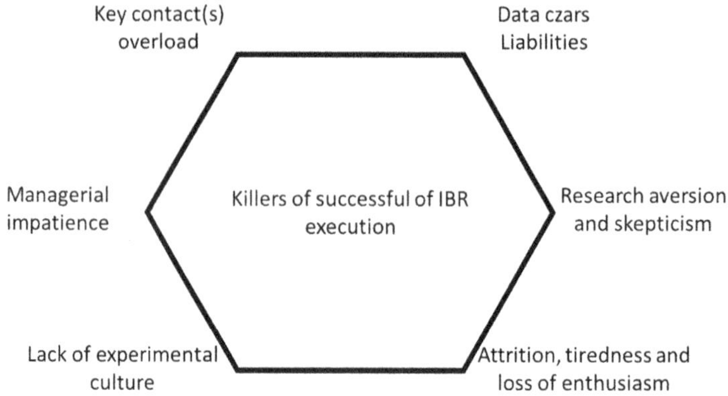

Figure 3.2: Factors hindering the successful IBR execution.

people in business tend to move more frequently than their academic counterparts. A key contact being promoted or leaving the company can pose a major challenge to the success of a project. Because uncertainty cannot be entirely forestalled, it is good practice to avoid overreliance on a key project contact by involving a network of stakeholders who have an interest in seeing that the project concludes successfully.

The country HR vice-president at a multinational consulting and IT company was wholly supportive of a project proposed by one of the authors, which soon materialized into a research contract. It quickly becoming clear, though, that C-level responsibilities were likely to render the VP a bottleneck, the research team agreed that all data requirement issues, liaison with other units, and so forth would be handled by a person assigned to the project team by the VP. The arrangement worked well; the VP was relieved of a continuous support role in the project and the HR specialist empowered to lead internal project activities and assure that the project progressed in the expected direction.

3.2.2 Managerial Impatience

Researchers and businesspeople live in worlds with different clock speeds. A year is an eternity for a company but a relatively short window of time for the execution of a research project. Businesspeople are inclined to disbelief when informed how long, from project conception to manuscript submission, it takes to (hopefully) publish a study's findings. Although likely to jump fast to an intervention to "see what happens," they may forget to collect data on core controls, disturbing proper evaluation of the effects of the intervention. People of action eager to get things done can be an asset unless their agitation detracts from quality and renders results unpublishable (unless, of course, you're on a career path to become a consultant!).

Staging the outcomes of a project by identifying "tangible" intermediate milestones can sometimes quell the impatience of business counterparts. In a project undertaken by one of the authors to understand how to staff B2B tendering teams at a telecommunications multinational in order to improve their sales effectiveness, it was soon realized that the process of integrating data from different databases would delay analysis by months. The team also realized, however, that the integrative database being developed, being a useful output for the company, could be introduced to the calendar as a formal delivery by ensuring that its format facilitated access to needed information.

It is also wise to remember that the degree of precision of analysis differs between business use and publication. Even in the absence of a suitable instrument for evaluating non-experimental data, analyses can be reported, acknowledging this limitation and recruiting the help of company experts to identify exogenous shocks or other valid instruments.

3.2.3 Lack of Experimental Culture

Although IBR is not necessarily about running field experiments, doing so certainly constitutes an important methodological option (Cook and Campbell, 1979). People in business, although they understand intuitively the benefits of experimentation, are not trained in the design of experiments. For many, to experiment means to "try something." Control groups, randomization, blocking, statistical control, power analyses, and testing levels of significance are concepts foreign to them, and they tend to lump multiple interventions together without any factorial design, which renders an intervention useless in the sense that there is no way to know what worked and what did not. These factors give rise to tensions between researchers and their business counterparts. There is no simple advice to be offered here. If an intervention is experimental, it must be made as rigorous as possible, with the caveat that to push ahead may necessarily entail some degree of compromise. The desire for perfect control may tempt a return to the lab, but the tradeoff would be the sacrifice of realism and generalizability. One suggestion to convince unfamiliar practitioners about the potential benefits of conducting organizational experiments is to highlight some success cases from the industry (e.g., Luca and Baserman, 2021) – see also Ibañez and Staats (2019) for more on how to use experiments effectively.

The creation of randomized treatment and control groups is a major impediment to the implementation of field experiments. Splitting a homogenous operating area into a treatment and control group can create technical problems. To create a control group for and intervention designed to introduce a new sales workflow system, for example, would involve having half the people use the new and half the old system, which perhaps uses a different database and interface with the ERP. Such problems are not insurmountable, but can be sufficiently complicated that managers prefer to roll interventions out to all target users. All that is possible in the face of these impediments is "damage control," for example, collecting sufficient control variables to parcel away possible threats to validity, or, in a large multi-unit organization, ferreting out is a unit sufficiently similar that did not implement the intervention (although this tack risks possible unobservable differences across the two units influencing results).

3.2.4 Data Czars

With respect to data, sourcing and access can be problematic in IBR projects. Researchers are well advised to keep in mind that between them and the data there is always at least one person, whether part of the project team or an employee of the organization hosting the study. A project team member is preferable given the exigencies of extracting data from corporate systems. An individual made responsible for data dumping who is not part of a project may not clearly understand the purpose of the target analyses. Data extracted incorrectly can generate errors that are time consuming to rectify, slowing a project and wasting resources. Errors detected too late constitute a worst-case scenario, casting a shadow of unreliability on a project and subjecting researchers' credibility to increased scrutiny by the organization or reviewers. The presence of a data "czar" who is resident on the project team not only helps to forestall errors, but also constitutes a store of knowledge about what resides in company archives that can open doors to opportunities to improve the empirical design of projects. The data czar in Salvador *et al.* (2021), for example, was the person who designed the transactive system in which the data needed by the team resided. The system having been built on an entity-relation database with dozens of tables, being able to call on its architect when dumping data was of inestimable value. No correction loops were ever needed, and the czar, having used the system intensively since its inception, was able to inform the research team about how the criteria for filling fields had changed over time.

Collection of new data can encounter myriad roadblocks including Human Resources departments, the General Data Protection Regulation (GDRP) in Europe, and corporate independent review boards and legal offices, which may impose their own clauses and restrictions on data collection efforts. The best way to deal with these problems is to write and NDA that allows you to use the data collected throughout the IBR study (or part of it) for publication purposes. Our advice is to specify in this agreement that you will disguise the identity of the company in your study, and that you will not publish certain descriptive information they may not want to publicize or indirectly reveal the identity of the firm. The company in a study of how subcontracting affected R&D project margins (Momcheva *et al.*, 2022), for example, did not want to share sensitive project margins data. The researchers resolved the company's concern by adding a fixed factor to the project margin data such that regression coefficients were not affected, but it was impossible to observe the precise point estimates of project margin at different levels of subcontracting.

Even with approvals in place, it may be necessary to solicit data from individuals who are not part of the research team or did not agree at the onset to provide data for the project. Persuasion is most effectively employed by demonstrating to these peripheral stakeholders the importance of their contribution and ways in which they will likely benefit from cooperating. People's willingness to participate in a study, especially if invited to do so at the outset, sometimes surprises researchers. A multinational firm recognized that information would need to be collected on a voluntary basis from technical project managers scattered across the five continents. Success in this endeavor was realized through the sponsorship of the firm's chief technology officer and credibility of the team of specialists that designed the data collection effort (Salvador and Madiedo, 2021).

3.2.5 Research Aversion and Skepticism

Managers averse or indifferent to research and collaboration with academics are not uncommon and can slow a project and cast doubt on its efficacy. It should be realized that the skepticism at the root of these attitudes often derives from stereotypes and ignorance. The perception of academic researchers as disconnected from reality and mainly interested in ivory tower speculation is common among businesspeople, and not without some basis, as is often the case with stereotypes. It's a mistake to attempt to overcome this misperception (assuming the researcher is not the sort that provides the basis for the stereotype) by behaving like a consultant or non-academic. Better to maintain the professional identity of an academic while striving to communicate your interest in understanding how to improve business practice.

Researchers sometimes find that business counterparts by whom they are respected and accepted as experts nevertheless remain skeptical that study findings will have any utility for their organizations. Among many sources of such skepticism is ignorance. While presenting at a practitioner conference the results of a study about factors that drive the speed of programmers (Bonet and Salvador, 2017), one of the authors noticed a participant sitting in the first row repeatedly dissenting with facial expressions and body language. Subsequently asked by the presenter the reason for the apparent disagreement, the participant snapped: "You cannot predict the time a programmer takes to do a task; it depends on a zillion factors." It became evident through a brief exchange that the individual lacked an appreciation for the concept of statistical control and its ability to decompose complex causal phenomena into multiple drivers. The skepticism of a manager at the research site presented with the same predictive algorithm largely evaporated when the algorithm was demonstrated to estimate task execution time better than planners. Bottom line: dispel skepticism by demonstrating that a methodology works.

3.2.6 Attrition, Tiredness, and Loss of Enthusiasm

Roles, people, teams, and organizations change in the course of an IBR project, and such dynamics must be acknowledged and managed to assure success. The problem of core team members leaving a project is well studied. That knowledge leaves a team with a person implies a liability. Because it is notoriously difficult, for instance, to find and bring up to speed a replacement for a project's data-czar, researchers are well advised to interact intensively with these individuals in order to become familiar with the locus of and procedures for extracting core data. The departure of the principal business counterpart can imply, in the worst case, the end of a project. But being unable to implement a planned intervention need not necessarily mean that a useful research project cannot be completed. The head of a North American homecare unit partnered with one of the authors to understand how work scheduling affects caregivers' performance, intending to use the findings from the analyses to implement scheduling constraints and evaluate the effects of the intervention. In the absence of support for the intervention in the wake of the sponsor's departure, the research team, continuing to work together to identify scheduling features that exerted a particularly negative effect on caregiver performance, produced a strong empirical research piece. Moreover, the team was able to exploit the expertise of the former sponsor, who had moved on to a different type of caregiver organization, to get a better sense of the empirical results (Momcheva *et al.*, 2022).

Burnout is frequently observed in contemporary organizations in which people are expected to respond to myriad bosses, requirements, and tasks. With little enough time to attend to the competing demands associated with their day-to-day responsibilities, they are likely to have difficulty mustering or sustaining enthusiasm for any outlying activity. Researchers themselves are subject to teaching commitments, revision deadlines, and other responsibilities that divert their attention. When momentum is lost, it can be extremely difficult to reinvigorate engagement by business partners. Awareness of these circumstances being key, there is value in scheduling weekly catch-up meetings to ensure that something is done, some progress made, or, conversely, that lack of action triggers early alarms.

Sustaining engagement is especially important for projects that involve stakeholders from more than one unit. If one unit routinely leads a project, others may be progressively left out and data and feedback from the marginalized units lost. This circumstance can potentially be averted by developing personal contacts with team members in other units who seem particularly interested in the project.

3.3 Validation of Insights

In IBR, as in any research, validity is a core concern for the researcher and should be as well for the practitioner. Implementing policies based on valid insights is certainly in the best interest of a business partner. The usual categories of measurement, internal and external validity, apply in this case. We discuss below six guidelines (see Figure 3.3) for increasing the validity of insights derived from IBR research. These guidelines can also be very useful for reviewers and editors as good criteria for evaluating the potential of an IBR manuscript.

3.3.1 Ex-Ante Analyses

A good way to avoid bad surprises in an IBR project is to assess available data before pursuing engagement. Doing so can impart a sense of reliability issues of all sorts in available measures. It may be, for instance, that the procedure for establishing a given measurement is not consistent across people or departments. Certainly, corrective measures are often possible, but to enact them the researcher must be first aware of their existence. This problem is aptly illustrated by an IBR study of Acute Coronary Infarction Syndrome was to be studied at a general hospital (Salvador and Escobar, 2013) meant to investigate how staffing

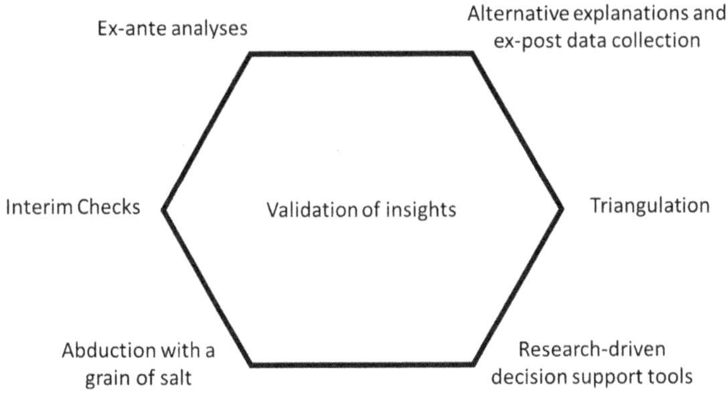

Figure 3.3: Enhancing the validity of IBR findings.

levels in the weekend affected patient mortality. Through a preliminary analysis we found a spike in mortality observed on Monday, which was suggestive that patient safety was affected by resource starving on the weekends. A subsequent check with the head of cardiology that the hospital's backbone Health Information System data, the source of the mortality information being used, was not updated on weekends, meaning that deaths that had occurred on Saturday and Sunday were recorded on Monday. Without this check we would not have been aware of such systematic bias in the mortality score we planned to use, which would have led to incorrect assessment of the intervention.

Similarly, it may be possible to reduce the cost of tracking the effects of an intervention by using available company information as proxies. For instance, the researchers were reminded by project team members that building complexity was a factor in a study of tendering effectiveness in a construction multinational, and was consequently, according to the specialists, more likely to win complex than simple projects. Yet no proxy for complexity (building shape, materials, etc.) seemed to affect tendering success. Intrigued, the researchers attempted to capture the latent concept of "building complexity" by constructing a factor score based on the different complexity indicators. To their surprise, the factor score was a significant predictor of tender success and retained as a control factor in the study of interventions aimed at improving the tendering process.

3.3.2 Interim Checks

A further advantage of IBR is that it requires researchers to continuously adjust their methods to improve the possibility of success (Oliva, 2019) and encourages evaluation of the plausibility of testable ideas. Too often researchers become more interested in the data than in the organization that produced it, leading to the generation of theory-driven hypotheses with little regard for how these explanations resonate with people who have direct knowledge of the process. The close interaction ensured by IBR not only discourages the formulation of off-the-mark hypotheses, but also provides insights into, among other things, alternative explanations, why things didn't work, and novel interventions that might warrant modification and testing.

3.3.3 Abduction with a Grain of Salt

According to the principle of abduction, when an empirical regularity is detected (i.e., a significant association is found) whose mechanism is unknown, a plausible causal mechanism can be identified using theory. This procedure is certainly useful, as it compels the researcher to compare what is observed but cannot be explained with what was found or argued by previous researchers. However, when engaging in IBR, a powerful alternative path towards theory-driven abduction is provided by the expertise of the practitioners. We cannot take the practitioner's explanation es valid a-priori. Yet, when the practitioner explanation dramatically diverges from the theory-driven one, an alarm should go on in the mind of the researcher, signaling the need to investigate better the unclear causal mechanism. The practitioner's feedback may just point us to look at a different literature to make sense of the mechanism. Perhaps, a literature stream that we did not know or did ignore because of personal preferences.

3.3.4 Alternative Explanations and Ex-Post Data Collection

The issue of alternative explanations can also arise in the review process. Theories abound, affording reviewers opportunities to propose explanations totally different from those provided by a researcher's own theory and business partners' insights. Researchers tightly connected to their business counterparts can solicit additional qualitative or quantitative data that can lead them to dismiss or incorporate alternative explanations. When a reviewer took issue with the postulated negative motivational effect in a study of work scheduling and absenteeism, for instance, suggesting instead that in the long run poorly conceived schedules make people sick, the researchers were able to return to the studied organization and collect data on which absences were due to, and re-run the analyses on those not associated with, medical reasons, which provided support for their hypotheses and strengthened the case for their motivational argument (Momcheva *et al.*, 2022).

3.3.5 Triangulation

Triangulation, the use of different methods, measures, or sources to investigate an empirical phenomenon, is a powerful means of providing convergent evidence that is gaining prominence as demonstrated by the increasing number of multiple-method papers being published. Close collaboration with practitioners paves the way to triangulating results in IBR studies. The effect of a novel work practice may be studied, for example, via a field experiment complemented by an internal survey that captures the unobserved perceptions of people relative to the intervention. Internal surveys can be a difficult sell in many companies, but such triangulation opportunities are more readily seized when trust has been gained and the potential benefits of collaboration demonstrated.

3.3.6 Research-Driven Decision Support Tools

IBR projects may involve efforts that do not feed directly into the research pipeline. A researcher interested in studying how an organization develops a digital decision-making tool and measuring its impact on performance may, in the process, help the organization to develop such a tool. This development activity could be framed as a reasonable "cost" of IBR. Keeping an open mind, however, the tool might be viewed as a potential source of further interesting research opportunities. Such a tool might, for example, generate an algorithm that forecasts expected task duration and hence be useful for planning and scheduling, or perhaps the variables included in the algorithm reveal a novel factor in task execution speed for which an explanatory model could be created and the algorithm used to assess the real impact of considering the factor in forecasting. IBR often takes twists and turns that open to receptive researchers doors to unexpected possibilities.

As observed, the six points presented in this section offer guidance for reviewers evaluating an IBR piece. These points highlight the importance of close collaboration between researchers and practitioners in strengthening the validity of the study. First, the reviewer could recommend additional *ex-ante analyses* to address potential concerns about systematic measurement errors or anomalous distributions. Second, the reviewer may become involved in *interim checks*, proposing alternative hypotheses and explanations that could be examined by the researcher in collaboration with field site personnel. Given the central role of the *abduction process* in IBR, this is an area where the reviewer should concentrate their attention, necessitating a clear account of the theory-evidence mismatch and the reasoning that led researchers to formulate new hypotheses. Furthermore, the reviewer should be vigilant about potential *alternative explanations* for the surprise findings often associated with IBR and require that they be empirically debunked—ideally. On the other hand, the reviewer can contribute to the validity of the study by requiring converging evidence of the findings through *triangulation* efforts, which are more feasible in an IBR context where collaboration between researchers and their business counterparts exists. Lastly, although the primary focus of an academic paper is the advancement of theory, the reviewer of an IBR piece should be aware that this type of research can offer rich and non-speculative insights on the implications of management research. This means that references to *decision support tools* developed by the researchers should not be hastily dismissed as irrelevant. Instead, they can provide valuable understanding of the connection between theory and practice.

3.4 Final Remarks on Research Methods for IBR

The question of which research tools to use is intentionally not addressed here because the authors believe there is nothing unique about IBR in this sense. IBR can employ any valid research tool (qualitative, survey, design, econometric, simulation, etc.) that is consistent with a research question and design. Generation of new theory being central in IBR, qualitative methods based on critical (not numerical) analysis of textual data often play an important role, yet the training in interviewing and qualitative coding and analysis techniques needed to effectively employ these methods is seldom provided in doctoral programs. How to report the results of qualitative research is a skill that must be learned to maximize the publication potential of IBR projects. But knowing only how to execute quantitative research restricts the range of questions that can be addressed through IBR. Hence, possessing an expanded methodological toolbox is essential. As the late Andrew van de Ven admonished University of Minnesota students for more than two decades, a fit must exist between the research question and the research tools used to address it. Without the proper tools, important questions surfaced by IBR interactions may go unaddressed and potentially important theoretical contributions be sacrificed. Professor van de Ven encouraged students to take follow-up methods courses in the methods identified as best fitting the questions underlying their dissertations. Exposing them to these thoughts early in doctoral programs will affect students' behavior as scholars by affording them sufficient time to take the methods courses needed to successfully pursue IBR or become engaged scholars generally.

The difference between a consultant and an engaged scholar pursuing IBR lies in the skill brought to the design and execution of interventions. The fluidity of problem situations and need to continually adjust interventions necessitate constant interaction between researchers and organizations. Further, as discussed in Section 2, standards of evidence require that data accessible to researchers be collected and documented in the most objective way possible. A formal process is needed to accommodate the collection and interpretation of data *while* an intervention is taking place in a rapidly moving project. For team members expected to provide evidence that justifies methodological changes or create new constructs that explain observed regularities, training in field methods (e.g., interviewing, case methods, action research, ethnography) is essential.

Students interested in IBR should not be dissuaded by the apparent superiority of laboratory experiments and mathematical modeling sometimes implied in doctoral training courses. Trade-offs between strengths and weaknesses are implicit in all research methods (McGrath *et al.*, 1982). Lab experiments, although they may be more conclusive about causality, are so at the cost of testing a real business situation in an entirely artificial setting (with a potential loss of external validity). Similarly, mathematical models that present theoretical arguments with extremely solid deductive reasoning are critically dependent on assumptions that need to be proven. The scientific acceptability of the many qualitative and quantitative research methodologies that can be used in the field to examine the validity and effects of an intervention depends exclusively on their appropriate application. Knowledge of these methods is prerequisite to post dissertation students becoming successful academics.

4

Evidence and Impact of IBR in OM

The previous section, which focused on strategies needed to conduct successful intervention-based research work, emphasized the importance of alignment between the research design and the research questions that guide a study. In this section, we examine some of the recently published IBR studies with the aim of explaining why the authors chose, and elucidating the insights derived from their use of, this method. Diverse fields and areas of application are represented in these articles including healthcare, process improvement, sourcing, and use of machine learning for forecasting. All begin with a clearly defined problem statement and stated strategy for addressing the issues, and effectively document the process that triggered a reframing of the problem, the exploration that led its resolution, and reflections on the theoretical generalizations and insights derived from the intervention. Both Mode 1 and Mode 2 applications of IBR in Operations Management are represented.

4.1 Examples

Our detailed explanations of how these papers came into existence include the stated purpose of the research and why the authors opted for an intervention approach, the surprising insights yielded by initial attempts at solutions, and what was learned that enabled the authors to generate theoretical insights beyond the study domain.

4.1.1 Example 1: Groop *et al.* (2017)

Groop *et al.* (2017) provide an illustrative example of the iterative learning process at work in IBR, capturing in particular the use of IBR in Mode 1, wherein interventions are employed to test a theory and the intervention strategy modified as results emerge.

Problem Situation

The authors engaged in a home care delivery system redesign effort aimed at improving how elderly people hosted in assisted living facilities access nurses and other care providers. With the elderly population increasing and healthcare costs rising, healthcare systems and insurance providers as well as other stakeholders (e.g., local governments) are investing in infrastructure for providing preventive health aids, such as transportation to care appointments, home visits to check on medication regimens, and assistance with daily chores. Helsinki city officials solicited from the authors help with what constitutes a wicked problem (Churchman, 1967) involving multiple stakeholders (e.g., healthcare workers, patients, hospitals, skilled nursing facilities) with potentially different interests. For instance, healthcare workers would focus on delivering better preventive care to the patient at their homes or post-acute care facilities and keeping them away from hospitals and skilled nursing facilities where they are prone to more infections and illness. Hospitals would focus on delivering safe care to the patients that can generate revenue while patients would prefer care offered at their convenience. To study such a problem that may have different objectives, the authors opted for an IBR approach that incorporated collaboration with the city officials and providers.

Initial Intervention

This research provides a vivid and instructive account of a prolonged problem-solving process in the messy swamp of practice characterized by ill-structured problems with many stakeholders with different objectives as explained earlier whose preferences often exhibit little overlap (Simon, 1973). Problem framing and problem definition becomes highly important in such scenarios. Solution development can be hampered not only by known problems, but also by unknown boundary conditions, and problem framing and definition may shift over time as insights evolve, new insights emerge, and key actors change. The authors characterize problem definition and solution design as an iterative process of exploring the problem, assessing stakeholder preferences, testing ("on paper"), and formulating and reformulating solutions.

In operational practice, problem solving involves more than choosing an appropriate OM theory and reconfiguring it to fit a particular context. The authors were trying to solve the specific problem of access by providers travelling to various patient locations throughout the city. A classic approach to this problem is the travelling salesman algorithm used to minimize travel times (Langevin *et al.*, 1990). The authors' reasoned that, by reducing non-value adding time associated to traveling across patients' locations, the fraction of available caregiver resources allocated to actual patient care would increase, thereby improving the quality of care. The travelling salesman algorithm thus represents the Theoretical Framework (T) that, as explained in Section 2, inspires the design of the initial intervention in the IBR cycle. Improving access by minimizing travel times, however, proved an unsatisfactory solution resulting in critical and non-critical visits being lumped together. The solution postponed care delivery to patients with critical needs, such as administration of medications and tests, in favor of delivering non-critical services (e.g., washing) to patients proximate to a previous appointment. That is, the Theoretical Framework (T) offered an overly simplified model of the real problem, thereby yielding unsatisfactory prescriptions.

Iteration and Results

The unexpected consequence of the initial scheduling resulting in poor solutions led the authors to work with stakeholders to understand the real need and frame the problem accordingly. The problem, they came to realize, was not minimizing travel times but ensuring the critical resources to be available to the elderly when needed. Appropriate interventions should take care of priorities in the allocation of tasks to resources: travel time became secondary to serving the most important needs (e.g., administering medications versus taking a patient for a walk). Following this realization, the authors abandoned the initial theoretical framework, drawing instead inspiration from the Theory of Constraints (Goldratt and Cox, 1984). Using the Theory of Constraints, the authors devised nurse scheduling heuristics that ensured that the bottleneck resource (i.e., the nurses) was first used where it added more value (i.e., priority patient care), leaving travel time reduction and serving non-priority patients as subordinate scheduling principles.

Contributions of This Research

This paper illustrates an important principle of IBR research, that when a theory fails to solve a problem the researchers are able to abductively derive new insights by collecting situated information about why the theoretically-derived intervention did not work. This corresponds to the Mode 1 approach of using IBR, wherein unanticipated results from the initial intervention force a reframing of the problem that, in turn, requires a new set of theories to update the intervention methodology. Initial failure in the selection of the theoretical framework was consequent to the assumptions of that framework (i.e., improve efficiency by minimizing travel times) not being reflected in idiosyncratic requirements of the system to be improved (i.e., improve effectiveness by ensuring that patients are served according to the severity of their conditions).

4.1.2 Example 2: Akkermans *et al.* (2019)

Problem Situation

The authors' investigation of how service firms design outsourcing contracts provides another example of Mode 1 IBR. Operations management research that endorses performance-based contracts that have either a final output deliverable (based, for example, on final quality, cost, or time) or process deliverable (based, for example, on some intermediate outcome or action) typically employs control theory (Ouchi, 1979), which assumes strict separation between the task of the buyer (i.e., the principal) and the supplier that executes the task (i.e., the agent). This is not the case in pure service settings, such as IT outsourcing, in which, because of the co-production of services, the performance of suppliers (i.e., contractors) depends greatly on that of buyers (Menor *et al.*, 2001). Service firms' consequent struggle to develop proper mechanisms to manage these relationships involves extensive negotiations that consume significant time and effort. Given the lack of guiding theory, the authors engaged in IBR to appropriate contract design.

Initial Intervention

One of the authors was part of a larger team that implemented service contracts for a Dutch telecommunication provider and its outsourced partner. Failure of the initial implementation of a service contract based on traditional performance milestones led the authors to explore the reasons for the ineffectiveness of traditional performance-based contracts. In collaboration with the telecommunication providers, they found out that buyer-supplier relationships in this instance had a larger number of interdependencies. They hence identified key performance indicators that jointly affect buyer and supplier performance and embedded these insights into the development of a new type of performance-based contract.

Iterations and Results

What the research team learned from the failure of the initial contract development effort informed the development of a new form of performance contract that involves key performance indicators (KPI) from buyer as well as supplier. The proposed approach, termed collaborative KPI, introduces decision transparency into the relationship and also takes into account the specific nature of individual tasks and how they are managed between the two parties. The new contract was effectively implemented and validated in another service setting as well.

The authors' reflection on their interventions suggests nuances in how service outsourcing relationships are best managed in such scenarios and propositions for applying these principles to the development of contracts in the service outsourcing context.

Contributions of This Research

This is an example of research begun as a traditional application of existing theory to solve a field problem. When extant theory failed to offer an effective solution, the authors, in collaboration with the problem owners, modified existing explanations out of which came the set of interventions. The paper makes an important theoretical contribution in fully leveraging ideas related to co-production of services long established (Roth and Menor, 2003) but not yet deployed to coordinate service provision.

In Mode 1 IBR, newer explanations generated by abductive reasoning when current explanations fail must be tested and evaluated before they can be generalized as nascent theory (Edmondson and McManus, 2007). In this case, the relative success of the contract that incorporated buyer KPIs provides tentative validation of the theoretical innovation.

4.1.3 Example 3: Anand *et al.* (2021)

Problem Situation

Notwithstanding abundant research on the benefits (e.g., Chandrasekaran *et al.*, 2012; Senot *et al.*, 2016; Tucker, 2007) and implementation (Tucker and Edmondson, 2003) of process improvement in healthcare, understanding of how to sustain process improvement initiatives in healthcare remains limited. Pursuit of this understanding requiring a longitudinal research design and deep knowledge of how a new process is designed and adapted by stakeholders that include physicians, nurses, and other providers is what led the authors to adopt IBR.

The manner in which the authors employ IBR in this study provides an example of a Mode 2 application, wherein interventions become a source of theory development (Oliva, 2019). Their interest in understanding how to enhance process improvement implementations in healthcare was directed specifically at improvement efforts related to discharge processes for kidney transplant patients. More than one-third of transplant patients have been documented to return to the hospital after surgery due to failure to adhere to discharge instructions. An average patient must follow more than 80 different instructions related to medications, testing, monitoring, and so forth, most delivered, often with significant variation, by nurses and physicians during the hospital stay. In communicating the requirement that patients consume 3 liters of water, for example, fluids are often substituted for water or 2 liters for 3 liters. Patients consequently end up not following the proper recovery regime at home, resulting in readmissions. The authors' examination of these processes revealed numerous previous improvement initiatives undertaken by the hospital, none of these initiatives sustained over time and failed to produce the intended effect on the patient care. Existing theories on process improvement implementation mostly focus on a homogenous group of individuals (i.e., providers, nurses) and do not provide guidance in situations wherein multiple stakeholders place several behavioral and systematic challenges to achieve sustainable improvement efforts, such as in the case of kidney transplants (i.e., patients, nurses, providers, social workers).

Initial Intervention

Working with more than 100 transplant providers including surgeons, nurses, clinical psychologists, and social workers at a major hospital, the authors identified a number of important roadblocks to change (e.g., Tyre and Von Hippel, 1997). They realized that existing change management theories, such as Kurt Lewin's "unfreeze change refreeze" framework (Schein, 1996) did not provide a working tool to enact process improvement in this context due to three major reasons. First, acknowledging the need to change, that is to "unfreeze" the focal process could signal to insurances potential liabilities—a situation the physician preferred to avoid. Second, the physicians were resisting change because of their skepticism towards the traditional change approach based on benchmarking other processes, on the basis of supposed uniqueness of the focal hospital process. Third, even when some change was attempted, physicians negatively reacted to the initial decline in performance that usually occurs during process improvement implementation (Netland *et al.*, 2015), hastily deeming the intervention unsuccessful. In addition, there were other challenges that were identified by the authors that included the difficulties in combining inputs from patients and providers in the initiation of process design, the need to adapt these process design when using them across a wide variety of patients and the need to sustain these PI changes. New theory was clearly called for.

Iterations and Insights

The authors identified two main countermeasures to meet the foregoing challenges that informed us beyond the current unfreeze-change-freeze arguments: the execution of experiments that worked as proof-of-concepts for improvement and the involvement of multiple stakeholders in process improvement. The initiation (unfreezing) challenge and overcoming initial decline in performance was overcome by performing evidenced-based experiments that demonstrated the existence of a problem in the focal process. Rather than claiming that a certain KPI is better for a benchmark process than for the target one—a fact that may be driven by contextual differences—within-process experiments showed to physicians how problems within their own unit compromised the unit's KPIs. Furthermore, establishing that the problem exists in their units made the physician group more aware of the need for change, despite the risks of signaling to third parties potential deficiencies of the established process. Because of this heightened awareness of the need for process improvement, the physicians also became more tolerant towards the initial decline in performance.

Having frontline employees develop their own standards allowed the employees to adapt these practices depending on the type of patients and hence minimized the adaptation in use challenge, and involving middle management in the process improvement initiative mitigated the sustainability challenge. Although previous studies of change management discuss the role of converting skeptics into believers in process changes (e.g., Adler *et al.*, 1999; Staats *et al.*, 2011), understanding of how to accomplish this in a context in which production and consumption of services occurs concurrently is limited, as is understanding of how to obtain real time feedback from customers (i.e., patients) to guide process adjustments. An example of the insights into how to manage these challenges yielded by the authors' research is capturing feedback from customers in parallel with the implementation of changes by nurses who can then refine them and thereby avoid missing performance targets.

The authors test the effectiveness of their intervention by comparing, using a difference-in-difference technique, patient data collected from the transplant unit with data from a similar unit that did not implement the intervention. Patient data included more than 571 kidney transplant recipients and more than 180 heart and liver transplant recipients who transitioned through the discharge teaching process before and after the process design. Fewer readmissions were observed among kidney patients discharged after the process design. Patient experience scores were also higher for the unit compared to other units discharging patients. Overall, the study findings suggest that interventions sustained over time offer new insights into the design of process improvements in healthcare.

Contributions of This Research

This research examined a complex problem, how to sustain process improvements, for which no particular theory offered a clear explanation. Sustaining process improvement requires a process theory to explain "How to make changes systematically to ensure they last over time." This initial decline in performance can give rise to skeptics who are primarily physicians that do not believe in the benefits from conducting these new changes. Common approaches such as benchmarking other areas within the organizations or looking at processes from other organizations did not work for creating buy-in among physicians. This created an important theoretical gap on how to generate buy-in among physicians when dealing with process improvement programs done by a heterogenous group of people (e.g., physicians, nurses, social workers etc.) The authors consequently pursued an understanding of the implementation process using an inductive field study. Applying both inductive and deductive logic (i.e., principles of abductive reasoning) to the problem resulted in the development of a new approach to process design. The authors began with existing theories from change management, the application of which resulted in modifications based on evidence from the site. This iterative approach to implementing change yielded new insights. Although IBR can stop with discovery, the authors undertook the additional step of testing to demonstrate the efficacy of the rolled-out intervention.

4.1.4 Example 4: Chun *et al.* (2022)

Problem Situation

Chun *et al.* (2022) is illustrative of an IBR study that incorporates both Mode 1 and Mode 2 reasoning. The authors' research on improving the transition of care for patients post-surgery began as a Mode 2 attempt to better understand how to transition care for patients who have undergone life altering surgeries. Building on work by Anand *et al.* (2021), the authors found that the first month after surgery is significant for discharged patients' health and wellness. Patients experience high anxiety and stress owing to fear of what can go wrong during these four weeks. The support available from hospitals' discharge coordinators via telephone and web messaging through EPIC does not significantly relieve patients' anxiety. Coordinators, moreover, being responsible for the care of several patients at a time, often experience burnout. There is a general lack of understanding of how to ensure patient safety and well-being during this four-week period. Current theory explaining patient transition, notably the Donabedian model of care (Anand *et al.*, 2021; Donabedian, 1988; Song and Veeraraghavan, 2018), emphasizes the role of nurses, physicians, social workers, and other providers in developing processes that minimize patient issues during the transitioning of care. That is, this model argues that structure of care, meant as having the right medical staff trained in discharging patients, improves the discharge processes, thus ultimately leading to better patient health post-surgery through minimized readmissions (Structure → Process → Outcomes). Evidence from the field, however, shows that despite good internal processes, patients continue to be readmitted due to complications that occur post discharge. That is, the process of care does not just stop within the hospital but also extends outside the hospital to ensure better compliance to discharge instructions. That is, Donabedian's model that has been traditionally looked at process of care within hospitals required modifications given the need to incorporate post-discharge factors (e.g., patient's routine for taking medications at homes etc.) that are beyond the control of healthcare workers Taken together, these factors make the problem of transition of care an ideal candidate for IBR since the current theories of transition of care do not explain how to accommodate self-monitoring routines when designing care.

Initial Intervention

To gain an understanding what happened during the first four weeks after discharge, the authors worked with the transplant team at a major hospital. They conducted interviews with transplant patients, nurses, coordinators, and families, and focus group sessions that brought together transplant patients who had received care over a period of 2 years (e.g., patients both recently discharged and who had surgery 2 years ago). Interactions within these groups revealed several interesting traits of discharged patients. The authors found, for example, that recently discharged transplant patients experienced higher anxiety about their health and wellness and were extremely comfortable listening to patients who had navigated the journey successfully. They further found that patients who had successfully navigated the transition of care had devised a number of best practices not ideally taught by nurses and coordinators. That evidenced-based care practices continued to be used, but were augmented by patients for ease of use, was an interesting finding. Their first six months of collaboration revealed to the authors and transplant team the value of using former transplant patients as peer-mentors to guide recently discharged patients. Although the use of mentors is not new to healthcare, using a standardized approach to offer mentoring yielded a number of benefits related to extending value creation outside the hospital and empowering patients to develop self-care routines.

Iterations and Results

Based on evidence from the initial iterations, the authors developed an intervention involving the use of peer mentors to empower patients.

Former transplant recipients, these mentors received, from the same transplant nurses and coordinators who instructed patients prior to discharge, training in a standard approach to helping other patients navigate the post-surgical stress. Using principles of standard work design (Anand *et al.*, 2021; Spear and Bowen, 1999), the mentors developed a four-week communication plan that included weekly telephone conversations with patients documented by both parties. The efficacy of this intervention was tested by the authors using a randomized-control design in which patients selected at random were placed into either a group that received the extra mentor care in addition to regular care or a group that received only regular care. Patients in the treatment group were matched to one of six mentors based on gender, race, and age, and the health and well-being outcomes of patients in both groups was tracked through the completion of the mentoring process.

Among results from the experiment, patients who transitioned using mentors exhibited lower levels of anxiety post discharge and, surprisingly, the readmission rate was higher for the treatment than for the control group. To understand the latter result, the authors returned to the transplant team and analyzed individual patient records (i.e., they pursued a Mode 1 line of inquiry elicited by a surprising result) to identify reasons for these earlier readmissions. It was discovered that earlier readmissions among patients in the treatment group were due to causes that can result in long-term injury to the transplanted organ; the mentoring process had enabled these patients to identify these issues, and return to the hospital, sooner. Early readmissions among control group patients the authors found to be due to not taking the correct medications, poor daily hydration, missing important labs, and other avoidable reasons.

Contributions of This Research

The insight from this research that not all readmissions are bad suggests that the current practice of penalizing hospitals for readmissions may not be optimal. This granular insight on readmissions, it should be noted, was a fruit of the intervention-based research method the authors employed, which entailed manually collecting, and classifying as preventable and unavoidable, data on what triggered readmissions. An important contribution of this study is the extension of the Donabedian Model to incorporate transition of care issues that need to be resolved for good healthcare delivery. The authors conclude that measures like patient anxiety post discharge are equally as important as other outcomes like patient satisfaction and readmissions. Much of the OM and healthcare literature ignores this transition period, the management of which is critical to patient well-being. Although the surprising result regarding readmissions yielded an important insight, it is difficult to generalize, leading the authors to suggest that more granular research in other settings is needed to understand the reasons for readmissions and inform policy makers' evaluation of this metric.

4.1.5 Example 5: Chuang *et al.* (2021)

Problem Situation

The authors were engaged by *Alpha*, one of the largest electronics distributors in the world, to develop a more accurate demand forecast over supplier lead time. *Alpha's* customers are large electronic manufacturing services (EMS) companies, mostly based in East Asia. Despite its size (revenues in excess of US$18 billion in 2018), *Alpha* has little power within the supply chain and its profit margins are tight and often compromised by high inventory holding and obsolescence costs, both attributable to seemingly unpredictable demand. The study focused on demand for 426 components from one major EMS client with 11 production plants. Only 14% of the items exhibited historically smooth demand, demand patterns for the remainder ranging from intermittent to erratic to lumpy (Syntetos *et al.*, 2005), all patterns for which demand is much more difficult to predict. In addition to weekly demand realizations, the downstream EMS client provides for each component a rolling forecast of expected demand or the next ten weeks (the suppliers' agreed lead time). The rolling forecast, however, did not improve over time (e.g., the forecast one week out was not more accurate than the forecast five weeks out) and management had decided that these forecasts were too noisy and unreliable for planning purposes. *Alpha* consequently employed a simple 8-week moving average (MA) of past weekly observations and multiplied it for the ten weeks of supplier lead time to develop a point estimate of the forecast.

Initial Intervention

In an initial attempt to improve the forecast, the authors deployed an array of time series modeling techniques that matched the demand characteristics of the 426 items in the test case. Each technique (the methods included sporadic demand forecasting capable of handling nonstationary demand processes and nonparametric methods based on neural networks) supposedly offered an improvement over the simple MA. Surprisingly, none of nine tested methods was able to perform, across the full set of test items, better than the 8-week MA used by *Alpha*, and the 8-week MA provided the best fit for the largest number of items.

Consideration of these results and further conversations with management led the authors to reassess the need to characterize weekly demand variations as opposed to providing a single forecast over lead time. More important, conversations with management revealed the need for a single robust method that could leverage information across items. These realizations led the authors to reframe the problem based on two data aggregation strategies, one to reduce temporal variance in the aggregation of demand over supplier lead time, the other to support integrated model estimation by performing cross-item aggregation across the 426 items. Under these revisited modeling assumptions, the authors engaged in an iterative process aimed at improving forecast accuracy.

Iterations and Results

With the aggregation assumptions in place, the authors created the appropriate features (i.e., independent data sources) to enable a machine-learning algorithm to detect patterns relevant to the prediction problem. Rather than focus on ad hoc transformation of available information, the approach preferred by data scientists, the authors chose to guide the design of the demand features using information they knew to be relevant to demand estimation (e.g., demand level, volatility, number of zeros, etc.) and elements to capture time invariant effects of the items, plants, and specific periods. Based exclusively on past historical data and fixed effects attributes, a simple random forest (RF) algorithm reduced the median forecasting error of the 8-week MA by 7.5% and the interquartile range of the errors by 6.6%.

A second iteration incorporated features of the EMS's rolling forecasts that were previously discarded. A final iteration improved the machine-learning algorithms. The model approved for roll-out improved the random model from the first iteration by further reducing the median error by 45% and the interquartile range of the errors by 39%. The improved forecast resulted in a 5% reduction of inventory holdings (a reduction of inventory value of US$3 million) without compromising the service level to the focal EMS. Although this EMS represented approximately 3% of *Alpha's* sales, the predictive methodology was deployed to all other major EMSs accounting for 56% of total sales.

Contributions of This Research

The intervention strategy described above can be mapped into multiple iterations of what Oliva (2019) calls Model 1 IBR, in which theories and methods are deployed to improve a problem situation. In the last section of the paper, the authors contrast their experience and results with existing guidelines for predictive machine learning, and derive insights beyond the specifics of the *Alpha* context. Specifically, they posit that combining temporal aggregation (that alleviates within volatility) and cross-item learning (that addresses between variability) can be a useful framework for capturing the non-smooth demand series common in manufacturing and demand settings, that a theory-informed approach to feature engineering, as opposed to the brute-force transformation proposed in statistical/machine learning, is not only more efficient but prevents the risk of blindly dropping theoretically relevant factors, and that their approach has "theoretic generalizability" (Meredith, 1998, p. 450). They further argue that their proposed guidelines will be useful in settings that share the attributes of the explored situation: supply for manufacturing processes in short product life markets and in which suppliers lack access to bills-of-materials and/or master production schedules.

4.2 Discussion

All these papers have three important elements in common. (1) The researchers actively engage in solving a problem in collaboration with practitioners. (2) The researchers' application of existing theories and frameworks surfaces inconsistencies that generate unexplainable surprises or unexpected results, and the subsequent engagement in a systematic enquiry about the surprises or unexpected results yields new insights into the problem that lead to the development of new theoretical insights. (3) The researchers generalize the insights from these iterations to develop a theoretical understanding that can be extended beyond the problem. These are sumarized, for the five examples, in Table 4.1.

IBR embraces all three elements as summarized above. Recall the discussion in Section 2 of using IBR to study complex problems. We believe there to be a high likelihood that all three elements will be realized when IBR is used to tackle such problems. This is how IBR differs from other activities like consulting, in which the focus is predominantly on element 1, and sometimes element 2. IBR is distinguished by taking the additional step of developing theoretical generalizations, that is, element 3.

We hope that this exercise of looking at various examples would give the readers the use of IBR as well as the insights that are developed through this method.

Table 4.1: Summary of select IBR papers published in the last 5 years

Papers	**Engagement with the Problem (Element 1)**	**Application of Existing Theories (Element 2)**	**Generation of New Theoretical Understanding (Element 3)**
Groop *et al.* (2017)	Researchers worked with the city, homecare agency, providers and patients to understand the challenges in delivering care.	Application of travelling sales-person problem for minimizing time to arrive at patient homes (Failed to explain the challenges)	General understanding on how value is created for elderly care and the importance of not looking at operational metrics alone
Akkermans *et al.* (2019)	Researchers worked with management team to design performance contracts between buyer and supplier firms.	Traditional outcome-based contracts applied and found to be less effective in service outsourcing.	Development of collaborating KPI contract that tracks both parties' metrics performs better. Can be generalized to other service outsourcing context
Anand *et al.* (2021)	Researchers worked with over 50 transplant providers (physicians, nurses, transplant coordinators and patients) for 3-years to understand the challenges of designing PI.	Traditional theories explaining PI implementation fails to explain the sustainability issue	Generating new insights on PI sustainability that requires overcoming four unique challenges in terms of initiating, avoiding initial performance decline, adaptation in use and sustaining PI beyond the team

Continued.

Table 4.1: Continued.

Papers	**Engagement with the Problem (Element 1)**	**Application of Existing Theories (Element 2)**	**Generation of New Theoretical Understanding (Element 3)**
Chun *et al.* (2022)	Researchers worked with over 15 former transplant patients and coordinators to understand the transition of care issues after patients are discharged.	Current transition of care theories fails to explain transitions beyond hospital boundaries.	Understanding the role of providers in developing standards for self-patient care through mentoring. Importance of looking beyond traditional outcomes such as 30-day readmissions when evaluating quality of care.
Chuang *et al.* (2021)	Researchers worked with demand managers of a large electronic distributor to improve the demand forecast accuracy of products with problematic – e.g., intermittent, lumpy, and erratic – demand distributions.	The problem had to be reframed once specialized methods to forecast sporadic and non-stationary demand patters failed to improved forecast accuracy over simple 8 weeks moving average. The reframing of the process to leverage temporal and cross-item aggregation led to machine learning tools that eventually made possible to exploit demand signals previously thought of as unreliable.	The development of data features based on theoretical insights form supply chain planning and forecasting methods was much more effective than the "brute force" approach of randomly generating transformation data transformations and interactions. Developed methodological guidelines have a broad area of application in settings with short product lives and where the supplier does not have access to the bill-of-materials.

5

Conclusion

We introduce in this monograph a new approach to conducting empirical research in OM. The need for engaged scholarship is well established and practiced in the OM community, yet reservations persist about the practice of co-creating knowledge with practicing managers. Interventions wherein the researcher is a change agent embedded in an organizational setting are not always encouraged for fear of influencing empirical results and contaminating the research design (Shadish *et al.*, 2001). However, we find that IBR, if designed appropriately, can help researchers challenge existing theoretical beliefs and can result in the creation of new and useful theories. It is from this perspective that we offer numerous insights on the use of IBR for advancing OM and management knowledge in general.

5.1 Importance of IBR for OM

IBR offers one template for empirical research that is alternative to unobtrusive data collection or to designing and executing field experiments. Its main strength lies in supporting abduction when existing theories fail to provide guidance in solving complex management problems. In these situations—wherein mismatches between theory and its practical application are likely—IBR offers the researcher heightened flexibility in collecting field evidence to generate novel theoretical insights that are parsimonious and plausible. By doing so, IBR often offsets incrementalism and fosters the generation of radical new insights, as evidenced by the numerous examples discussed in Section 4. Thus, IBR contributes to the theory building enterprise by putting theory to work in real problem-solving situations, unlike other theory-building approaches such as case study research. By the same token, the IBR researcher is prompted to develop new OM theory that moves away from borrowing general management and sociological theories, which are often remote from problem-solving concerns. We do not claim that IBR must be used to develop new theories, but that it affords a way to account for practice in the development of theories.

A further unique feature of IBR is that the researcher can act upon the empirical setting by interacting with its different actors, taking part in decision-making and even execution of activities, as well as in the design and execution of the intervention. This obtrusiveness of the researcher, who is no longer an "external" unobtrusive observer, may lead some to confuse consulting with IBR. This is not the case. Certainly, both consultants and IBR researchers have an interest in helping with solving real problems. They also both have an interest in drawing lessons from the intervention that are potentially portable to other settings. However, the IBR researcher has a distinctive scholarly interest in moving beyond "lessons learned" to identify novel underlying mechanisms that push the envelope of extant theory. It is in this important abductive stage of developing theoretical propositions that makes IBR different than consulting.

Among the most significant benefits of IBR is the opportunity it affords researchers to develop immediate insights into theory, practice, and the education of business professionals. This "Trifecta" model is common in Harvard Business School's philosophy of research. By way of example, Anand *et al.*'s (2021) study of sustainable process improvement in healthcare focused on understanding why its effects fail to be sustained over time and the role of healthcare workers in developing sustainable process improvements. Asked by leaders at a large medical center to explore the problem in the context of transplant care, the authors developed over the course of two years an intervention that was subsequently evaluated on the basis of data obtained from transplant recipients. The study contributed to the quality management literature rich theoretical insights not only into how to sustain process improvement, but also into the role of patients as co-owners of the care delivered during their hospital stay. Working with the providers, the authors were able through additional data collection to identify a number of unique patient challenges. Their findings resulted in the publication of three additional articles, one (Chandrasekaran *et al.*, 2016), relating insights that differed slightly on the role of patient anxiety and standards of care in reducing readmissions, published in a medical journal and thereby facilitating immediate dissemination of this new knowledge to the practitioner community. The others, a pedagogical case study used to instruct MBA students in how to develop standards of care in the presence of customers (Gadkari and Chandrasekaran, 2012) and a *Harvard Business Review* article (Chandrasekaran and Toussaint, 2019) focused on leadership behaviors requisite to successful organizational transformation.

We argue that, through consideration of the relevance of the problem and engagement with practice, IBR constitutes a useful, albeit not the only, approach to developing a Trifecta (theory, practice, and management education) of knowledge creation and impact. Recent years have seen numerous questions raised about the role of business schools in creating relevant knowledge (Augier and March, 2011). Engagement through IBR is one way to address concerns voiced by a number of business school deans about the need for academic research to be practically relevant.

5.2 Promising Areas for IBR Work

Despite its promise, IBR is not a panacea for all areas of OM research. Its large set up cost (e.g., securing access and organizational commitment) and delays in obtaining useful data for the theorizing process, suggest that IBR is best suited to studying contemporary challenges that may not be readily explained by existing theory. Decarbonization of the economy, population health management, precision medicine, AI ethics, and Human-AI decision making are among the areas in which traditional explanations may not hold. Consider, for example, in the area of AI ethics, the role of big-data and AI in generating business challenges that, although they do not pose any legal or regulatory issues, can create ethical issues. Examining such issues from a stakeholder theory perspective (Freeman, 1984) doesn't always elucidate gray areas of ethics because the concept of what constitutes an ethical AI decision is still emerging. In such areas, researchers can employ an IBR approach to engage with practitioners (e.g., data scientists) in order to better understand the gray areas and approaches that can be deployed to help manage them. Similarly, little is known about how humans and AI can interact to co-create decisions that are better than either could generate independently, sometimes referred to as Human-AI symbiosis (Jarrahi, 2018). It is increasingly common for human designers and AI technologies to interact. Take, for example, designers using 3D printing/additive manufacturing capabilities to augment designer efforts to improve design for manufacturing capabilities. Whereas current theories around, for instance, socio-technical systems don't really provide a good explanation for how humans and AI can cocreate new knowledge, IBR offers novel insights into how researchers studying contemporary issues that are not well understood can create practical knowledge as well as contribute to the development of new theories.

5.3 Final Caveat

IBR is not without significant risks, however. For instance, not all engagements with complex problems yield a mismatch between theory and practice, and simply exploring an interesting problem and finding a mismatch between existing theory and practice does not constitute IBR. Understanding why existing theory doesn't explain practice and how this finding can be extrapolated outside the problem is the distinguishing characteristic of IBR. A researcher investigating a problem with practitioners may find existing theories to provide sufficient explanation and thus render the experience less productive. IBR is consequently not necessarily an ideal research strategy for doctoral students or early career scholars given the time pressures of job markets and tenure.

That said, for such researchers as are inclined to adopt this method, we recommend a portfolio approach of adopting an IBR study design as a complement to traditional deductive or inductive designs (e.g., field experiments, large data analyses, case studies, etc.). Doctoral candidates with multiple papers in their dissertations, by including one that reflects an IBR design, demonstrate that they are researching interesting and impactful problems while minimizing the risk that attends the approach.

We certainly encourage tenured scholars as well to engage in IBR work that can expand their impact on the field and contribute to business practice through the Trifecta model referenced above. It is our hope that this monograph serves to introduce OM scholars to our varied insights into IBR and generate a movement around pursuing more problem-driven empirical research in collaboration with practitioners.

References

Ackoff, R. (1981). "The art and science of mess management". *Interfaces*. 11(1): 20–26. DOI: 10.1287/inte.11.1.20.

Adler, P. S., B. Goldoftas, and D. I. Levine (1999). "Flexibility versus efficiency? A case study of model changeovers in the Toyota production system". *Organization Science*. 10(1): 43–68. DOI: 10.1287/orsc.10.1.43.

Akkermans, H., W. van Oppen, F. Wynstra, and C. Voss (2019). "Contracting outsourced services with collaborative key performance indicators". *Journal of Operations Management*. 65(1): 22–47. DOI: 10.1002/joom.1002.

Anand, G., A. Chandrasekaran, and L. Sharma (2021). "Sustainable process improvements: Evidence from intervention-based research". *Journal of Operations Management*. 67(2): 212–236. DOI: 10.1002/joom.1119.

Argyris, C., R. Putnam, and D. M. Smith (1985). *Action Science: Concepts, Methods and Skills for Research and Intervention*. San Francisco: Jossey-Bass.

Ashby, E. (1967). "The future of the 19th century idea of a university". *Minerva*. 6(1): 3–17. DOI: 10.1007/BF01101602.

Augier, M. and J. March (2011). *The Roots, Rituals, and Rethorics of Change: North American Business Schools After the Second World War*. Redwood City, CA: Stanford University Press.

Bell, J. A. and J. F. Bell (1980). "System dynamics and scientific method". In: *Elements of the System Dynamics Method*. Ed. by J. Randers. Cambridge, MA: Productivity Press. 3–22.

Bell, J. A. and P. M. Senge (1980). "Methods for enhancing refutability in system dynamics modeling". *TIMS Studies in the Management Sciences*. 14(1): 61–73.

Bonet, R. and F. Salvador (2017). "When the boss is away: Manager-worker separation and worker performance in a multisite software maintenance organization". *Organization Science*. 28(2): 244–261. DOI: 10.1287/orsc.2016.1107.

Bunge, M. (1967). *Scientific Research*. New York: Springer-Verlag.

Cachon, G. P. and R. Swinney (2011). "The value of fast fashion: Quick response, enhanced design, and strategic consumer behavior". *Management Science*. 57(4): 778–795. DOI: 10.1287/mnsc.1100.1303.

Chandrasekaran, A., G. Anand, L. Sharma, T. Pesavanto, M. L. Hauenstein, M. Nguyen, M. Gedkari, and S. Moffatt-Bruce (2016). "Role of in-hospital care quality in reducing anxiety and readmissions of kidney transplant recipients". *Journal of Surgical Research*. 2005(1): 252–259. DOI: 10.1016/j.jss.2016.05.032.

Chandrasekaran, A., C. Senot, and K. K. Boyer (2012). "Process management impact on clinical and experiential quality: Managing tensions between safe and patient-centered healthcare". *Manufacturing & Service Operations Management*. 14(4): 548–566. DOI: 10.1287/msom.1110.0374.

Chandrasekaran, A. and J. S. Toussaint (2019). "Creating the culture of continuous improvement". *Harvard Business Review*. 5(24): 2–5.

Checkland, P. B. (1981). *Systems Thinking, Systems Practice*. Chichester, UK: Wiley.

Checkland, P. B. (1985). "From optimizing to learning: A development of systems thinking for the 1990s". *Journal of the Operational Research Society*. 36(9): 757–767. DOI: 10.1057/jors.1985.141.

Chuang, H. H. C., Y. C. Chou, and R. Oliva (2021). "Cross-item learning for volatile demand forecasting: An intervention with predictive analytics". *Journal of Operations Management*. 67(7): 828–852. DOI: 10.1002/joom.1152.

Chun, Y., S. L. Harris, A. Chandrasekaran, and K. Hill (2022). "Improving care transitions with standardized peer mentoring: Evidence from intervention based research using randomized control trial". *Journal of Operations Management.* 68(2): 185–214. DOI: 10.1002/joom.1170.

Churchman, C. W. (1967). "Wicked problems". *Management Science.* 14(4): 141–142.

Clark, K. B. (1989). "Project scope and project performance: The effect of parts strategy and supplier involvement on product development". *Management Science.* 35(10): 1247–1263. DOI: 10.1287/mnsc.35.10.1247.

Coase, R. H. (1937). "The nature of the firm". *Economica.* 4(16): 386–405. DOI: 10.1111/j.1468-0335.1937.tb00002.x.

Cook, T. D. and D. T. Campbell (1979). *Quasi-Experimentation: Design & Analysis Issues for Field Settings.* Boston: Houghton Mifflin.

Croson, R. and K. Donohue (2006). "Behavioral causes of the bullwhip effect and the observed value of inventory information". *Management Science.* 52(3): 323–336. DOI: 10.1287/mnsc.1050.0436.

Cyert, R. M. and J. G. March (1963). *A Behavioral Theory of the Firm.* Englewood Cliffs, NJ: Prentice-Hall.

Deming, W. E. (1982). *Out of the Crisis.* Cambridge, MA: MIT Press.

Denyer, D., D. Tranfield, and J. E. van Aken (2008). "Developing design propositions through research synthesis". *Organization Studies.* 29(3): 393–413. DOI: 10.1177/0170840607088020.

Descartes, R. (1998). *Discourse on Method (1637).* Indianapolis: Hackett Publishing Co.

Donabedian, A. (1988). "The quality of care: How can it be assessed?" *JAMA.* 260(12): 1743–1748. DOI: 10.1001/jama.1988.03410120089033.

Eckhardt, J. and J. C. Wetherbe (2014). "Making business school research more relevant". Retrieved May 30th, 2023. URL: https://hbr.org/2014/12/making-business-school-research-more-relevant.

Edmondson, A. C. and S. E. McManus (2007). "Methodological fit in management field research". *Academy of Management Review.* 32(4): 1155–1179. DOI: 10.5465/amr.2007.26586086.

Fisher, M. L. (1997). "What is the right supply chain for your product?" *Harvand Business Review.* 75: 105–117.

Fisher, M. L., J. H. Hammond, W. R. Obermeyer, and A. Raman (1994). "Making supply meet demand in an uncertain world". *Harvard Business Review*. 72: 83–93.

Forrester, J. W. (1961). *Industrial Dynamics*. Cambridge, MA: MIT Press.

Freeman, R. E. (1984). *Strategic Management: A Stakeholder Approach*. Boston: Pitman Publishing.

Gadkari, M. and A. Chandrasekaran (2012). "The emergency department (ED) at the Burton group of hospitals—Application of lean and value stream mapping". In: *Sague Business Cases*. London: SAGE Publications, Ltd.

Goldratt, E. M. and J. Cox (1984). *The Goal: A Process of Ongoing Improvement*. Great Barrington, MA: North River Press.

Gordon, R. A. and J. E. Howell (1959). *Higher Education for Business*. New York: Columbia University Press.

Groop, J., M. Ketokivi, M. Gupta, and J. Holmström (2017). "Improving home care: Knowledge creation through engagement and design". *Journal of Operations Management*. 53: 9–22. DOI: 10.1016/j.jom.2017.11.001.

Gulati, R. (2007). "Tent poles, tribalism, and boundary spanning: The rigor-relevance debate in management research". *Academy of Management Journal*. 50(4): 775–782. DOI: 10.5465/amj.2007.26279170.

Hanson, N. R. (1958). *Paterns of Discovery*. Cambridge, UK: Cambridge University Press.

Hurley, P. J. (2000). *A Concise Introduction to Logic*. 7th ed. Belmont, CA: Wadsworth.

Ibañez, M. R. and B. R. Staats (2019). "Field experiments in operations management". *INFORMS TutORials in Operations Research. Operations Research & Management Science in the Age of Analytics*: 1–16.

Jarrahi, M. H. (2018). "Artificial intelligence and the future work: Human-AI symbiosis in organizational decision making". *Business Horizons*. 61(4): 577–586. DOI: 10.1016/j.bushor.2018.03.007.

Juran, J. M. (1994). "The upcoming century of quality". *Quality Progress*. 27(8): 29.

Kuhn, T. S. (1970). *The Structure of Scientific Revolutions.* 2nd ed. Chicago: University of Chicago Press.

Langevin, A., F. Soumis, and J. Desrosiers (1990). "Classification of travelling salesman problem formulations". *Operations Research Letters.* 9(2): 127–132. DOI: 10.1016/0167-6377(90)90052-7.

Langley, A. (1999). "Strategies for theorizing from process data". *Academy of Management Review.* 24(4): 691–710. DOI: 10.2307/259349.

Langley, A., C. Smallman, H. Troukas, and A. H. van de Ven (2013). "Process studies of change in organization and management: Unveiling temporality, activity and flow". *Academy of Management Journal.* 56(1): 1–13. DOI: 10.5465/amj.2013.4001.

Locke, J. (1996). *An Essay Concerning Human Understanding (1776).* Indianapolis: Hackett Publishing Co.

Luca, M. and M. H. Baserman (2021). *The Power of Experiments: Decision Making in a Data-driven World.* Cambridge, MA: MIT Press.

Madiedo, J. P., A. Chandrasekaran, and F. Salvador (2020). "Capturing the benefit of worker specialization: Effects of managerial and organizational task experience". *Production and Operations Management.* 29(4): 973–994. DOI: 10.1111/poms.13145.

Mantere, S. and M. Ketokivi (2013). "Reasoning in organization science". *Academy of Management Review.* 38(1): 70–89. DOI: 10.5465/amr.2011.0188.

Mcauliffe, W. H. B. (2015). "How did abduction get confused with inference to the best explanation?" *Transactions to the Charles S. Peirce Society.* 51(3): 300–319. DOI: 10.2979/trancharpeirsoc.51.3.300.

McGrath, J. E., J. Martin, and R. A. Kulka, eds. (1982). *Judgment Calls in Research.* Newbury Park, CA: Sage.

Menor, L. J., A. V. Roth, and C. H. Mason (2001). "Agility in retail banking: A numerical taxonomy of strategic service groups". *Manufacturing & Service Operations Management.* 3(4): 273–292. DOI: 10.1287/msom.3.4.273.9969.

Meredith, J. (1998). "Building operations management theory through case and field research". *Journal of Operations Management.* 16(4): 441–454. DOI: 10.1016/S0272-6963(98)00023-0.

Mohr, L. B. (1982). *Explaining Organizational Behavior.* San Francisco: Jossey-Bass.

Momcheva, A., F. Salvador, and E. Avgerinos (2022). "Subcontracted labor mix in project teams: Evidence from high-tech project teams". *Manufacturing & Service Operations Management.* 24(5): 2722–2740. DOI: 10.1287/msom.2022.1125.

Monge, P. P. (1990). "Theoretical and analytical issues in studying organizational processes". *Organization Science.* 1(4): 406–430. DOI: 10.1287/orsc.1.4.406.

Nair, S., M. K. Malhotra, and S. L. Ahire (2011). "Towards a theory of managing context in Six Sigma projects: An action research investigation". *Journal of Operations Management.* 29: 239–548. DOI: 10.1016/j.jom.2010.11.014.

Netland, T. H., J. D. Schloetzer, and K. Ferdows (2015). "Implementing corporate lean programs: The effect of management control practices". *Journal of Operations Management.* 36: 90–102. DOI: 10.1016/j.jom.2015.03.005.

Oliva, R. (2001). "Tradeoffs in responses to work pressure in the service industry". *California Management Review.* 43(4): 26–43. DOI: 10.2307/41166099.

Oliva, R. (2003). "Model calibration as a testing strategy for system dynamics models". *European Journal of Operational Research.* 151(3): 552–568. DOI: 10.1016/S0377-2217(02)00622-7.

Oliva, R. (2019). "Intervention as a research strategy". *Journal of Operations Management.* 65(7): 710–724. DOI: 10.1002/joom.1065.

Oliva, R. (2020). "On structural dominance analysis". *System Dynamics Review.* 36(1): 8–28. DOI: 10.1002/sdr.1647.

Oliva, R., H. Gebauer, and J. Brann (2012). "Separate or integrate? Assessing the impact of separation between product and service business on service performance in product manufacturing firms". *Journal of Business to Business Marketing.* 19(4): 309–333. DOI: 10.1080/1051712X.2012.647797.

Oliva, R. and R. Kallenberg (2003). "Managing the transition from products to services". *International Journal of Service Industry Management.* 14(2): 160–172. DOI: 10.1108/09564230310474138.

Oliva, R. and J. D. Sterman (2001). "Cutting corners and working overtime: Quality erosion in the service industry". *Management Science*. 47(7): 894–914. DOI: 10.1287/mnsc.47.7.894.9807.

Oliva, R. and N. H. Watson (2011). "Cross-functional alignment in supply chain planning: A case study of sales and operations planning". *Journal of Operations Management*. 29(5): 434–448. DOI: 10.1016/j.jom.2010.11.012.

Oreskes, N., K. Shrader-Frechette, and K. Belitz (1994). "Verification, validation, and confirmation of numerical models in earth science". *Science*. 263: 641–646. DOI: 10.1126/science.263.5147.641.

Ouchi, W. G. (1979). "A conceptual framework for the design of organizational control mechanisms". *Management Science*. 25(9): 833–848. DOI: 10.1287/mnsc.25.9.833.

Peirce, C. S. (1955). *Philosophical Writings of Peirce*. Edited by Buchler J. New York: Dover.

Peirce, C. S. (1965). "Collected papers of Charles Sanders Pierce Vol. 5". In: *Pragmatism and Pragmaticism*. Ed. by C. Hartshorne and P. Weiss. Cambridge, MA: Harvard University Press.

Pentland, B. P. (1999). "Building process theory with narrative: From description to explanation". *Academy of Management Review*. 24(4): 711–724. DOI: 10.2307/259350.

Poole, M. S., A. H. van de Ven, K. Dooley, and M. E. Holmes (2000). *Organizational Change and Innovation Processes: Theory and Methods for Research*. Oxford, UK: Oxford University Press.

Reynes, S. L., J. M. Bartunek, and R. L. Daft (2001). "Across the great divide: Knowledge creation and transfer between practitioners and academics". *Academy of Management Journal*. 44(2): 340–355. DOI: 10.2307/3069460.

Rittel, H. W. and M. M. Webbet (1973). "Dilemmas in general theory of planning". *Policy Sciences*. 4(2): 155–169. DOI: 10.1007/BF01405730.

Roth, A. V. and L. J. Menor (2003). "Insights into service operations management: A research agenda". *Production and Operations Management*. 12(2): 145–164. DOI: 10.1111/j.1937-5956.2003.tb00498.x.

Rozeboom, W. W. (1997). "Good science is abductive, not hypothetico-deductive". In: *What If There is No Significance Test?* Ed. by L. L. Harlow, S. A. Mulaik, and J. A. Steiger. Mahwah, NJ: Lawrence Erlbaum Associates Inc.

Runkel, P. J. and M. Runkel (1984). *A Guide to Usage for Writers and Students in the Social Sciences.* Totowa, NJ: Rowman & Allanheld.

Salvador, F., C. Alba, J. P. Madiedo, A. Tenhiälä, and E. Bendoly (2021). "Project managers' breadth of experience, project complexity, and project performance". *Journal of Operations Management.* 67(6): 729–754. DOI: 10.1002/joom.1140.

Salvador, F. and D. Escobar (2013). "Más rápido, más eficiente y mejor: Un estudio del proceso asistencial de pacientes con Síndrome Coronario Agudo". *Advanced Series on Problem-Driven Research: Healthcare Industry.* 1(1): 12–71.

Salvador, F. and J. P. Madiedo (2021). "Enabling globally distributed projects: Effects of project interface match and related technical experience". *Production and Operations Management.* 30(4): 1052–1081. DOI: 10.1111/poms.13292.

Schein, E. H. (1987). *The Clinical Perspective in Fieldwork.* Newbury Park, CA: Sage.

Schein, E. H. (1996). "Kurt Lewin's change theory in the field and in the classroom: Notes toward a model of managed learning". *Systems Practice.* 9(1): 27–47. DOI: 10.1007/BF02173417.

Schneiderman, A. M. (1988). "Setting quality goals". *Quality Progress.* 21(4): 51–57.

Schön, D. A. (1987). *Educating the Reflective Practitioner.* San Francisco: Jossey-Bass.

Senot, C., A. Chandrasekaran, P. T. Ward, A. L. Tucker, and S. D. Moffatt-Bruce (2016). "The impact of combining conformance and experiential quality on hospitals' readmissions and cost performance". *Management Science.* 62(3): 829–848. DOI: 10.1287/mnsc.2014.2141.

Shadish, W. R., T. D. Cook, and D. T. Campbell (2001). *Experimental and Quasi-Experimental Designs for Generalized Causal Inference.* Boston: Houghton Mifflin.

Shah, R. and P. T. Ward (2007). "Defining and developing measures of lean production". *Journal of Operations Management.* 25(4): 785–805. DOI: 10.1016/j.jom.2007.01.019.

Simon, H. A. (1967). "The business school: A problem in organizational design". *Journal of Management Studies.* 4(1): 1–16. DOI: 10.1111/j.1467-6486.1967.tb00569.x.

Simon, H. A. (1973). "The structure of ill structured problems". *Artificial Intelligence.* 4(3–4): 181–201. DOI: 10.1016/0004-3702(73)90011-8.

Simon, H. A. (1988). "The science of design: Creating the artificial". *Design Issues.* 1(2): 67–82. DOI: 10.2307/1511391.

Song, H. and S. Veeraraghavan (2018). "Quality of care". In: *Handbook of Healthcare Analytics: Theoretical Minimum for Conducting 21st Century Research on Healthcare Operations.* Ed. by T. Dai and S. Tayur. 79–108.

Spear, S. and H. K. Bowen (1999). "Decoding the DNA of the Toyota production system". *Harvard Business Review.* 77: 96–108.

Spencer, L., L. Anderson, and P. Ellwood (2022). "Interweaving scholarship and practice: A pathway to scholarly impact". *Academy of Management Learning & Education.* 21(3): 422–448. DOI: 10.5465/amle.2021.0266.

Staats, B. R., D. J. Brunner, and D. M. Upton (2011). "Lean principles, learning, and knowledge work: Evidence from a software services provider". *Journal of Operations Management.* 29(5): 376–390. DOI: 10.1016/j.jom.2010.11.005.

Sterman, J. D., R. Oliva, K. Linderman, and E. Bendoly (2015). "System dynamics perspectives and modeling opportunities for research in operations management". *Journal of Operations Management.* 39–40(1): 1–5. DOI: 10.1016/j.jom.2015.07.001.

Strauss, A. and J. Corbin (1990). *Basics of Qualitative Research: Grounded Theory Procedures and Techniques.* Newbury Park, CA: Sage.

Sutherland, J. W. (1975). *Systems; Analysis, Administration and Architecture.* New York: van Nostrand.

Syntetos, A. A., J. E. Boylan, and J. Croston (2005). "On the categorization of demand patterns". *Journal of the Operational Research Society.* 56(5): 495–503. DOI: 10.1057/palgrave.jors.2601841.

Tang, C. S. (2017). "OM forum—Three simple approaches for young scholars to identify relevant and novel research topics in operations management". *Manufacturing & Service Operations Management*. 19(3): 338–346. DOI: 10.1287/msom.2017.0633.

Tranfield, D. and K. Starkey (1998). "The nature, social organization and promotion of management research: Towards policy". *British Journal of Management*. 9(4): 341–353. DOI: 10.1111/1467-8551.00103.

Tucker, A. L. (2007). "An empirical study of system improvement by frontline employees in hospital units". *Manufacturing & Service Operations Management*. 9(4): 492–505. DOI: 10.1287/msom.1060.0156.

Tucker, A. L. and A. C. Edmondson (2003). "Why hospitals don't learn from failures: Organizational and psychological dynamics that inhibit system change". *California Management Review*. 45(2): 55–75. DOI: 10.2307/41166165.

Tyre, M. J. and E. Von Hippel (1997). "The situated nature of adaptive learning in organizations". *Organization Science*. 8(1): 71–83. DOI: 10.1287/orsc.8.1.71.

van Aken, J. E. (2005). "Management research as a design science: Articulating the research products of mode 2 knowledge production in management". *British Journal of Management*. 16(1): 19–36. DOI: 10.1111/j.1467-8551.2005.00437.x.

van Aken, J. E., A. Chandrasekaran, and J. Halman (2016). "Conducting and publishing design science research: Inaugural essay of the design science department of the journal of operations management". *Journal of Operations Management*. 47–48: 1–8. DOI: 10.1016/j.jom.2016.06.004.

van de Ven, A. H. (1989). "Nothing is quite so practical as a good theory". *Academy of Management Review*. 14(4): 486–489. DOI: 10.5465/amr.1989.4308370.

van de Ven, A. H. (2007). *Engaged Scholarship: A Guide for Organizational and Social Research*. Oxford, UK: Oxford University Press.

van de Ven, A. H. and P. E. Johnson (2006). "Knowledge for theory and practice". *Academy of Management Review*. 31(4): 802–821. DOI: 10.5465/amr.2006.22527385.

Printed in the USA
CPSIA information can be obtained
at www.ICGtesting.com
LVHW011759311223
767819LV00004B/452

9 781638 282242

van Mieghem, J. A. (2013). "OM forum—Three Rs of operations management: Research, relevance, and rewards". *Manufacturing & Service Operations Management*. 15(1): 2–5. DOI: 10.1287/msom.1120.0422.

Weick, K. E. (1989). "Theory construction as disciplined imagination". *Academy of Management Review*. 14(4): 516–531. DOI: 10.2307/258556.

Womack, J. P., D. T. Jones, and D. Ross (2007). *The Machine that Changes the Word: The Story of Lean Production*. New York: Simon and Schuster.

Yin, R. K. (2003a). *Applications of Case Study Research*. 2nd ed. Thousand Oaks, CA: Sage.

Yin, R. K. (2003b). *Case Study Research: Design and Methods*. 3rd ed. Thousand Oaks, CA: Sage.